APPLE WATC... USER GUIDE

A Complete User Manual with Step By Step Instruction For Beginners And Seniors To Learn How To Use The New Apple Watch Series 8 Like A Pro With WatchOS 9 Tips & Tricks

BY

HERBERT A. CLARK

Table of Contents

INTRODUCTION

Welcome to Apple Watch Series 8, the versatile wrist companion that can help you be more active, track health info, and most importantly connect you with your loved ones—with or without your iPhone.

This manual will help you find all the great things the Apple Watch Series 8 can do.

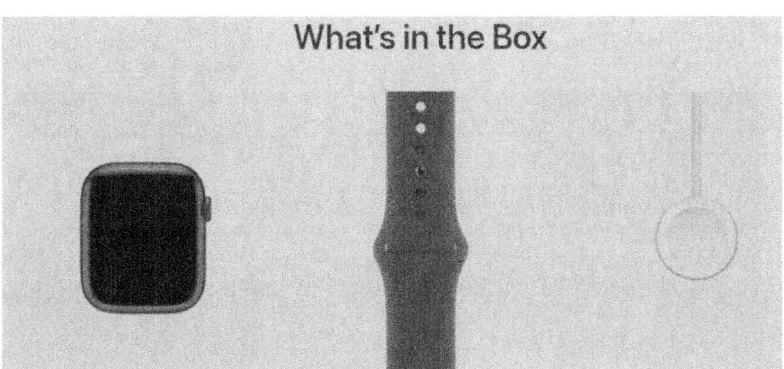

FEATURES OF APPLE WATCH SERIES 8

Design

The Apple Watch Series 8 did not receive a design update. It still uses the same round, square design as the foregoing generations and comes in 41 mm & 45 mm sizes.

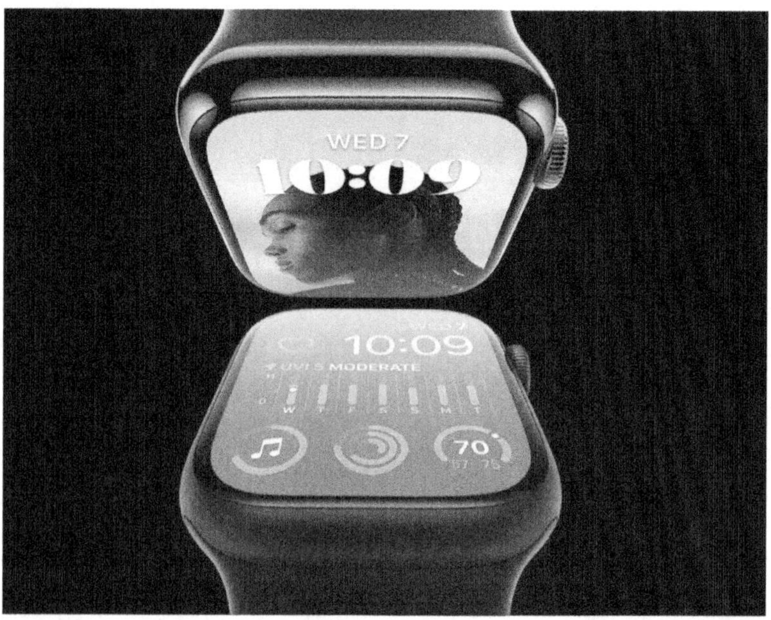

The Apple Watch has smooth, rounded edges around the screen and it weighs between 32g & 51.5g, depending on case size & material.

The smartwatch has a black ceramic & crystal back which houses 4 photodiodes & 4 LED clusters to make it easy for health-monitoring features like ECG & blood oxygen monitoring to function.

There's a Digital Crown on the watch's side which can be used for navigation & scrolling, and a side button that can be used to confirm Apple Pay purchases, access emergency services, etc.

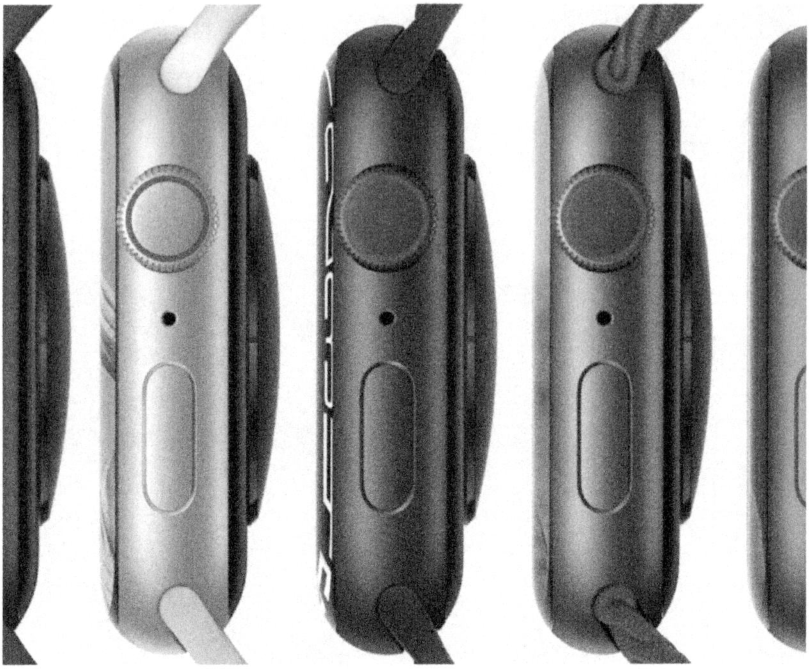

Colours & materials

The new Apple Watch is available in three different materials: stainless steel & aluminum. The aluminum model is the cheapest, while the stainless steel model is more expensive.

The aluminum model colours include (PRODUCT) RED, Silver, Starlight, & Midnight. While, the Stainless steel model colours include Space black, Graphite & Gold.

41 mm

- Aluminum: 32g
- Stainless steel: 42.3g

45 mm

- Aluminum: 38.8g
- Stainless steel: 51.5g

Water & dust resistance

The new Apple Watch features IP6X dust resistance for use in places such as the beach or deserts, and WR50 water resistance, rated for immersion in water as deep as 164 feet.

Since it is rated for 50 meters of water immersion, the Apple Watch Series 8 can be used in the ocean or a swimming pool. It is only suitable for shallow water activity and cannot be used for scuba diving, or other activities that involve high-speed water or deep water submersion.

Health Features

The new Apple Watch offers health monitoring features like a 3rd-gen optical heart-rate sensor that calculates metrics such as a very high heart rate, resting heart-rate, & calories burned. You can also use the electric heart rate sensor to take ECG, while the infrared light & LEDs allows users to track blood oxygen level. An inbuilt gyroscope

& accelerometer allows other important health-related features like Fall detection to function properly.

Your smartwatch can detect irregular, high & low heart rates. The Apple Watch can also detect health issues like AFib and send you notifications when it detects anomalies.

Battery life

The Watch Series 8 offers an “all-day” 18-hour battery life from a single charge, which can be increased to about 36 hours with the Low Power Mode.

SETUP YOUR APPLE WATCH

Before setting up your smartwatch you need to update your iPhone to the latest version of iOS, enable Bluetooth and connect your iPhone to a cellular or WiFi network.

Switch on your watch and wear it

Long-press the side button until you see the Apple symbol on your screen. Then wear your smartwatch on your wrist.

Bring your watch near your iPhone

Wait for the **"Use iPhone to setup Apple Watch"** notification to pop-up on your phone, then touch the **Continue** button. If you don't see this message, enter the Watch application on your iPhone, touch All Watches, then touch the **Add Watch** button.

If this is your personal watch, touch the **Setup For Myself** option.

Make sure your Apple Watch & iPhone are close while you follow these steps.

Scan the animation

Set your phone in a way that the watch face can be seen in the view finder

If you cannot utilize the camera, or the animation does not appear, or your phone cannot read it, touch the **Pair Manually** button, and then follow the instructions.

Setup as new or restore from backup

If this is your first Apple smartwatch, touch the **Setup as New Apple Watch** option. If prompted, update your smartwatch to the latest watchOS version.

If you have paired another Apple smartwatch with your current phone, you will see a screen that says "Make This Your New Watch". Touch App & Data and Settings to see how Express Set up is going to configure your new smartwatch. Then touch Continue. Touch the **Customize Settings** option if you want to choose how your new smartwatch will be configured. Then select one of the backups from another previous Apple Watch to restore. Or, if you want to fully personalize your watch's settings, touch the **Setup as New Apple Watch** option.

Select the wrist you want to wear your smartwatch on and then touch the **Continue** button

Go through the Terms & Conditions and then touch the **Agree** button.

Log in with your Apple ID

If prompted, type your Apple ID login code. If you're not prompted, you can login any time from the Apple Watch application: Touch the **General** button> Apple ID, then log in

If the Find My feature is not setup on your phone, you will be prompted to enable Activation Lock. If you see the Activation Lock screen, it means your smartwatch is already linked to an Apple ID. You'll need to insert the Apple ID's email address & password to continue setup.

Create a login code

You can decide to skip this part, but you'll need a passcode if you want to use features like Apple Pay on your watch.

On your phone, touch **Create Pass code** or **Add Long Pass-code**, then type the new passcode on your smartwatch. To skip this part, touch the **Don't Add Passcode** button.

Personalize your settings

Choose your desired text size.

If you did not make use of Express Set up, your smartwatch would show you the settings it shares with your Phone. If you activate features like Location Services, Diagnostics, Find My, & WiFi Calling for your Phone, these settings automatically activate on your smartwatch.

Next, add or update information like your date of birth to ensure your Health & Fitness data are correct. You can also activate health notifications like noise level and more.

Setup cellular & Apple Pay

You can setup cellular if your Apple Watch is a cellular model.

Next, you will be prompted to setup Apple Pay by adding a credit, debit, or transit card. Then your phone will walk you through features like Always On Display and your preferred application view.

Allow your devices to synchronize

Your smartwatch will show the watch face when the pairing process is complete. Keep your phone near your watch so that the two devices can continue to synchronize information in the background

Unpair your smartwatch

- Enter the Watch application on your phone.
- Touch the **My Watch** tab, then touch **All Watches** at the upper part of your display.
- Touch the Info icon beside the Apple Watch you want to unpair, and then touch the **Unpair Apple Watch** button.

Pair more than one watch

You can connect another Apple smartwatch the same way you connected the first one. Or adhere to the directives below:

- Enter the Watch application on your phone.

- ❖ Touch the **My Watch** tab, then touch **All Watches** at the upper part of your display.
- ❖ Touch the **Add Watch** button, then adhere to directives on your screen.

Quickly switch to another Apple smartwatch

Your phone will detect the paired Apple Watch you are putting on and automatically connect to it. Just wear another Apple Watch and raise your hand.

You can also select an Apple smartwatch manually:

- ❖ Enter the Watch application on your phone.
- ❖ Touch the **My Watch** tab, then touch **All Watches** at the upper part of your display.
- ❖ Disable Auto Switch

To know if your smartwatch is connected to your phone, long-press the bottom of your watch screen, swipe up to reveal the Controls Center, then look for the Connection Status logo

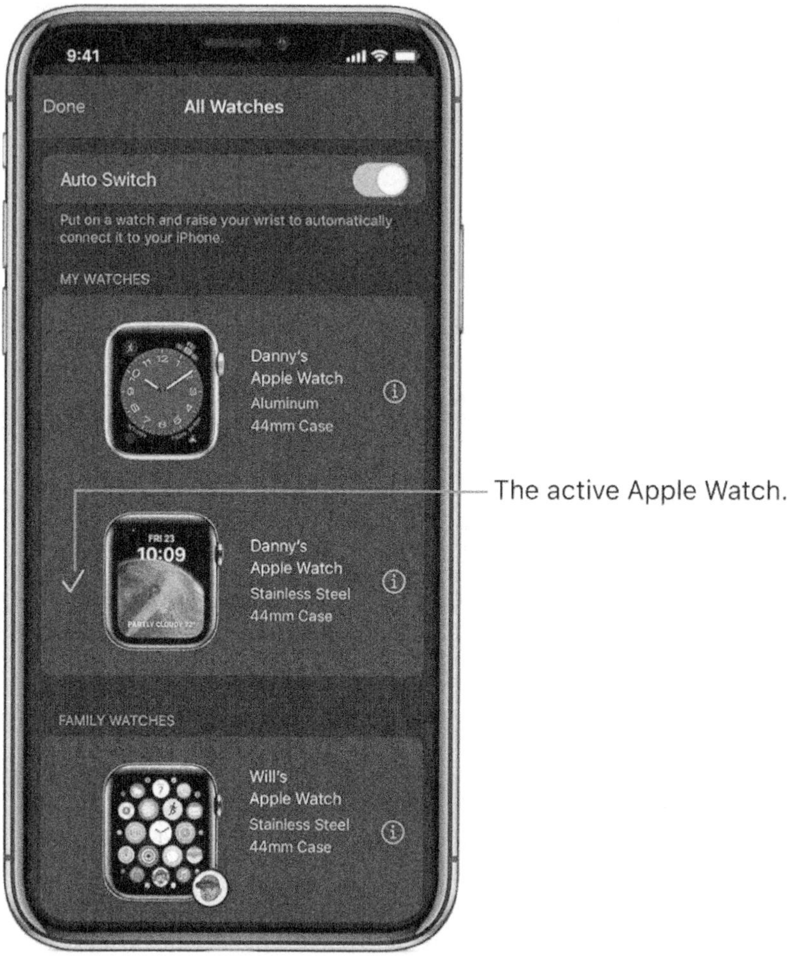
9:41
Done
All Watches
Auto Switch
Put on a watch and raise your wrist to automatically connect it to your iPhone.
MY WATCHES
Danny's
Apple Watch
Aluminum
44mm Case
FRI 23
10:09
Danny's
Apple Watch
Stainless Steel
44mm Case
FAMILY WATCHES
Will's
Apple Watch
Stainless Steel
44mm Case
The active Apple Watch.

SETUP A FAMILY MEMBER'S WATCH

Switch on your watch and wear it

Long-press the side button until you see the Apple symbol on your screen. Then wear your smartwatch on your wrist.

Bring your watch near your iPhone

Wait for the **"Use iPhone to setup Apple Watch"** notification to pop-up on your phone, then touch the **Continue** button. If you don't see this message, enter the Watch application on your iPhone, touch All Watches, then touch the **Pair New Watch** button.

Touch the **Setup for Family Member** option, then touch the **Continue** button on the next screen.

Scan the animation

Set your phone in a way that the watch face can be seen in the view finder

If you cannot utilize the camera, or the animation does not appear, or your phone cannot read it, touch the **Pair Manually** button, and then follow the instructions.

Then touch the **Setup Apple Watch** button

Setup a passcode

Touch the **Agree** button on the Terms & Condition screen, then select your watch's text size

After that, create a pass-code to safeguard your data

Choose a family member

Pick the family member that's going to be using the Apple Watch. If you can't find them in the list, touch the **Add New Family Member** button.

Type the person's Apple ID login code, then touch **Next**

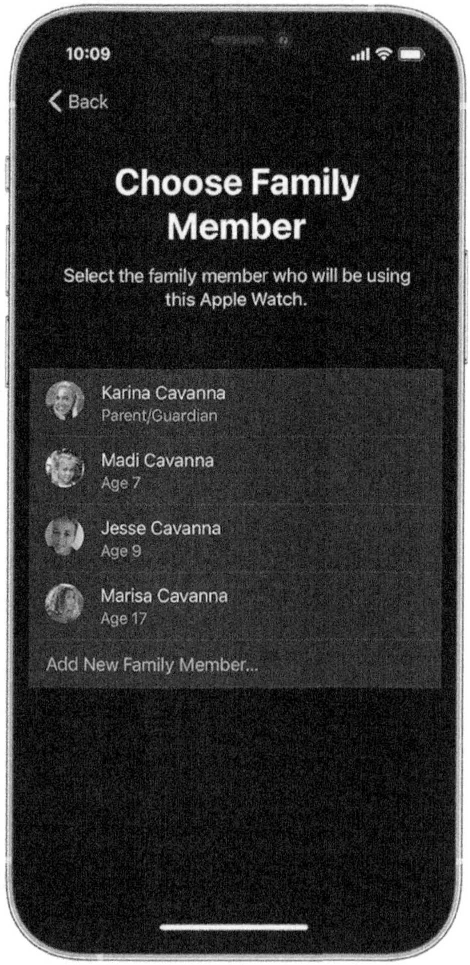

Activate Ask to buy

Activate the **Ask to Buy** feature if you want the person that's going to be using the watch to always ask for approval before they can download or purchase items on the Apple Watch.

Setup WiFi & cellular

Add the Apple Watch to your cellular plan or do it later

After that, choose whether to share your WiFi with the smartwatch.

Activate other features

On the following screens, choose whether to activate & setup additional Apple Watch features. These include Siri, Health Data, Emergency SOS, Workout Route, and more.

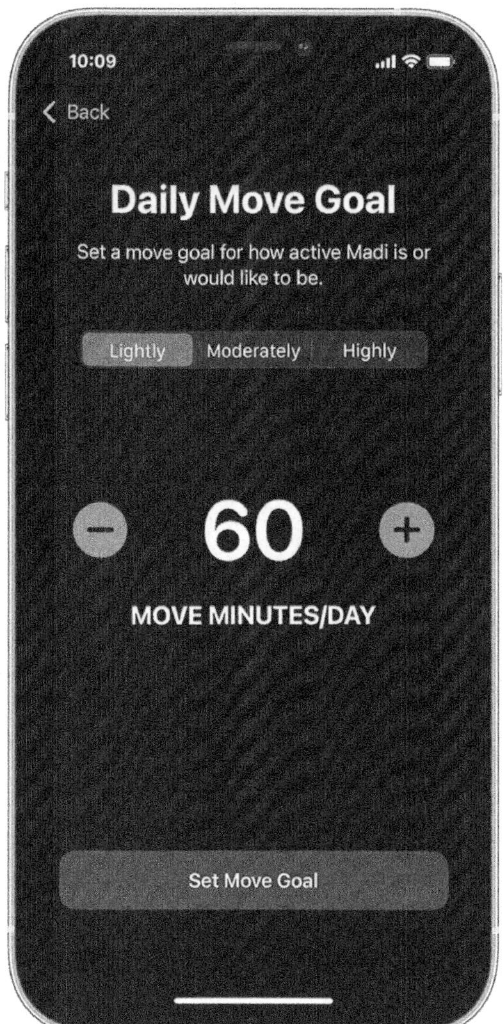

Setup shared contacts & Schooltime

You will now be prompted to setup contacts that will be available on your smartwatch. To allow this, you need to enable Contacts in iCloud. On your iPhone, enter the Settings application> [your name] > iCloud and make sure Contacts is enabled.

Then you can select people from your Contacts application to share on the watch.

Lastly, set a Screen Time passcode for the smartwatch, and activate Schooltime. When you are done, touch **Ok** to start making use of the Apple Watch.

WATCH BASICS

Apple Watch Series 8

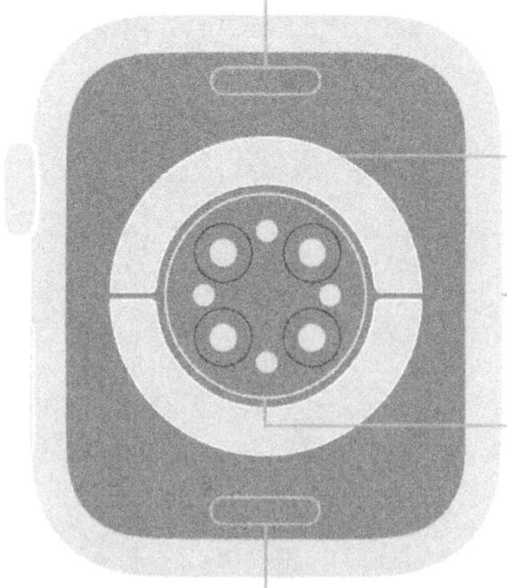

Switch your smartwatch on & off

- Switch on: Long-press the side button till you see the Apple symbol on your screen (you may see a black screen at first).

- Switch off: Long-press the side button till the sliders pop up, touch the Power button at the upper right, and then drag the Power Off slide to the right end.
  When your smartwatch is off, you can long-press the Digital Crown to view the time.

Tip: You cannot switch off your smartwatch while it's charging. You have to disconnect the watch from the charger first before you can switch it off.

Charge your watch

- Put the charger or charging cord on a leveled surface in a well-ventilated place.
- Connect the charging cable to the adapter.

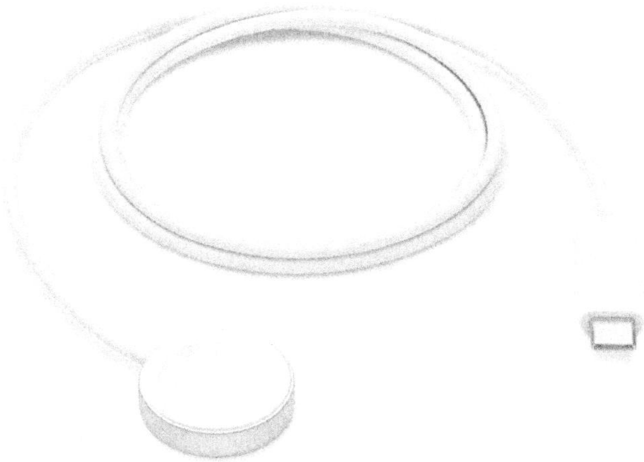

- Plug the adapter into a power socket.
- Put the Magnetic charger on the back of your smartwatch.

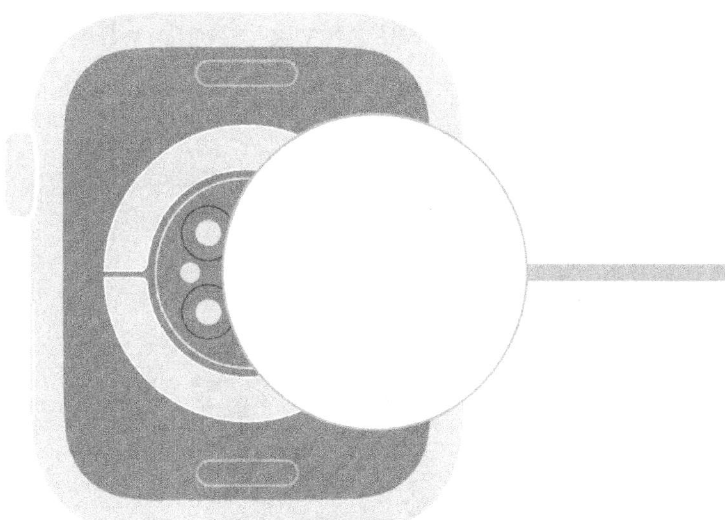

The concave end of the charger would magnetically snap to the back of your smartwatch and hold it in place.

Your smartwatch will play a chime when it starts charging and a charging icon will appear on the watch face

Apple Watch app

With the Watch application on your iPhone, you can personalize watch faces, change settings, customize the Dock, install applications, etc.

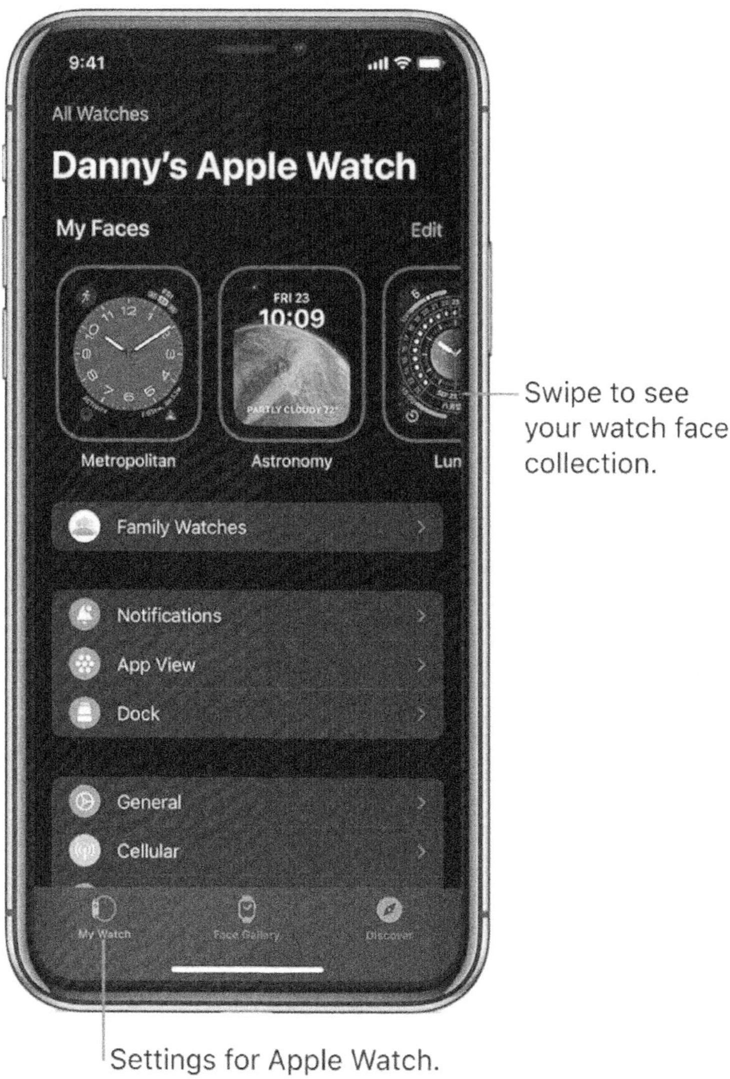

❖ Touch the Apple Watch application icon on your iPhone to open the application.
❖ Touch the **My Watch** button to see your watch's settings.

Watch gestures

Use the following basic gestures to interact with your smartwatch:

❖ Touch: Use one of your fingers to gently touch the screen.

❖ Swipe: Move one of your fingers across your watch screen—right, down, left, or up.

❖ Drag: Move one of your fingers across your watch screen without lifting the finger.

❖ Long-press: Touch & hold an item in an application or Controls Centre to perform quick actions.

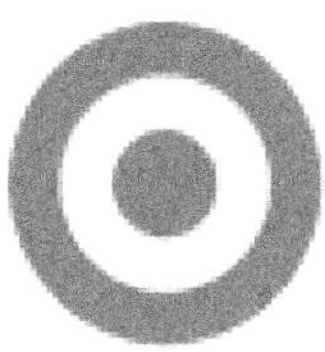

Open apps on your watch

Your smartwatch comes with different apps that can help you keep track of your health, workout, and more. To launch an application, just press the Digital Crown, then touch the app. Press the Digital Crown once more to return to your Watch's Home Screen. You can also download apps from the Application Store on your smartwatch.

Wake your watch display

You can wake your watch display in the following ways:

- ❖ Raise your hand. Your smartwatch goes back to sleep when you put your wrist down.
- ❖ Touch the screen or press the Digital Crown.
- ❖ Rotate the Digital Crown.

If you do not want your smartwatch to wake up when you raise your hand or rotate the Digital Crown, head over to the Settings application on your watch, touch Display and Brightness, then deactivate Wake on Crown Rotation & Wake on Wrist Raise.

Check remaining power

To check how much power your watch has left, simply long-press the bottom of your watch screen, then swipe up to reveal the Controls Center.

Save power

You can activate Low Power Mode to save your battery life. Activating Low Power Mode will turn off background blood oxygen & heart rate measurements, Always-On Display, and heartrate notifications.

Note: The Low Power mode will be deactivated when your watch is 80 percent charged.

❖ Long-press the bottom of your watch screen, then swipe up to reveal the Controls Center

- Touch the battery percentage, and then activate Low Power Mode.
- Scroll down, and then touch Turn On Low Power Mode to confirm your choice.
  You can touch the **Turn On For** option, then select On for 3 Days, On for 2 Days, etc.

Deactivate Low Power mode to go back to normal power mode.

Check how long it has been since you last charged your watch

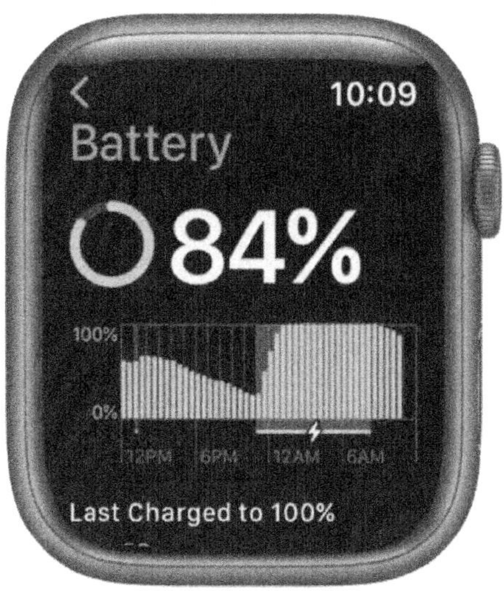

- Enter the Settings application on your watch.

❖ Touch Battery.
The battery screen shows the battery percentage, recent battery charge history, and the last time the battery was charged.

Check battery health

❖ Enter the Settings application on your watch.
❖ Touch Battery, then touch Battery Health.

Always On

The Always-On feature allows your watch to display the watch face & time, even when you put your wrist down. When you raise your wrist, your smartwatch functions fully.

- Enter the Settings application on your smartwatch.
- Touch Display and Brightness, then touch Always-On.
- Activate Always On, then touch the following options to set them up:
  - Show Complications Data: select the complications that will display information when your hand is down.
  - Show Notification: select the notifications that will be visible when your hand is down.
  - Show apps: select the application that will be visible when your hand is down.

Go back to clock face

You can set how long your smartwatch stays before returning to the clock face from an open application.

- Enter the Settings application on your watch.

- Head over to General > Return to Clock, then scroll down and select when you want your smartwatch to go back to the clock face: After an hour, After 2 minutes, or Always.
- You can also press the Digital Crown to go back to the clock face.

Wake up to last activity

For some applications, you can programme your smartwatch to go back to where you were in the application before it went to sleep.

- Enter the Settings application on your watch.
- Head over to General > Return to Clock, scroll down and touch an application, then activate Return to App

To go back to the clock face, simply stop what you are doing in the application, for instance, cancel a timer, or stop a podcast.

Keep your smartwatch display on longer

- Enter the Settings application on your smartwatch.
- Touch Display and Brightness, touch Wake Duration, then touch Wake for 70 Seconds

Connect your watch to Wi-Fi

- Long-press the bottom of your watch's screen, swipe up to reveal the Controls Centre
- Long-press the Wi-Fi button , then touch an available network.
- If a password is needed, carry out any of the below:
    - Type the password using your keyboard.
    - Touch the Password icon , then select a password.
- Click Join.

Forget a network

- Long-press the bottom of your watch's screen, swipe up to reveal the Controls Centre
- Long-press the Wi-Fi button , then touch the network you joined.

- ❖ Touch the **Forget This Network** button

Unlock your watch

You can unlock your watch by inserting your passcode, or you can set your watch to automatically unlock when you unlock your iPhone.

- ❖ Enter your passcode: Wake your watch, and then type your pass-code.
- ❖ Unlock your watch when you unlock your iPhone: Enter the Watch application on your phone, touch **My Watch**, touch Passcode, and then activate **Unlock with iPhone**.

  Your phone and your watch have to be within the standard Bluetooth range (about 33ft). If Bluetooth is deactivated on your smartwatch, insert the passcode on your watch to unlock it.

Change your passcode

You can follow these steps to change the passcode you created when setting up your watch:

❖ Enter the Settings application on your smartwatch.
❖ Touch Passcode, then touch Change Passcode and adhere to the directives on your screen.

To use a passcode longer than 4 digits, enter the Settings application on your smartwatch, touch the Passcode button, and then deactivate Simple Passcode.

To turn off the passcode, enter the Settings application on your smartwatch, touch the

Passcode button, and then touch Turn Off Passcode

Lock your watch manually

- Long-press the bottom of your watch screen, then swipe up to reveal the Controls Center
- Touch the Lock button .

Note: To lock your watch manually, you have to deactivate Wrist detection. (On Apple Watch, enter the Settings application, touch Passcode, and then deactivate Wrist Detection.)

You will need to insert your passcode when next you try to use your watch.

Erase your watch after ten unlock attempts

To safeguard your data if your watch is lost or stolen, you can programme your watch to delete its data after ten consecutive attempts to unlock it with an incorrect passcode.

- Enter the Settings application on your smartwatch.
- Touch Passcode, then activate Erase Data

Choose a region or language

If you have setup your iPhone to use multiple languages, you can pick the language that appears on your watch.

- Enter the Apple Watch application on your phone.

- Touch **My Watch,** head over to General, touch Language and Region, touch Custom, then select a language.

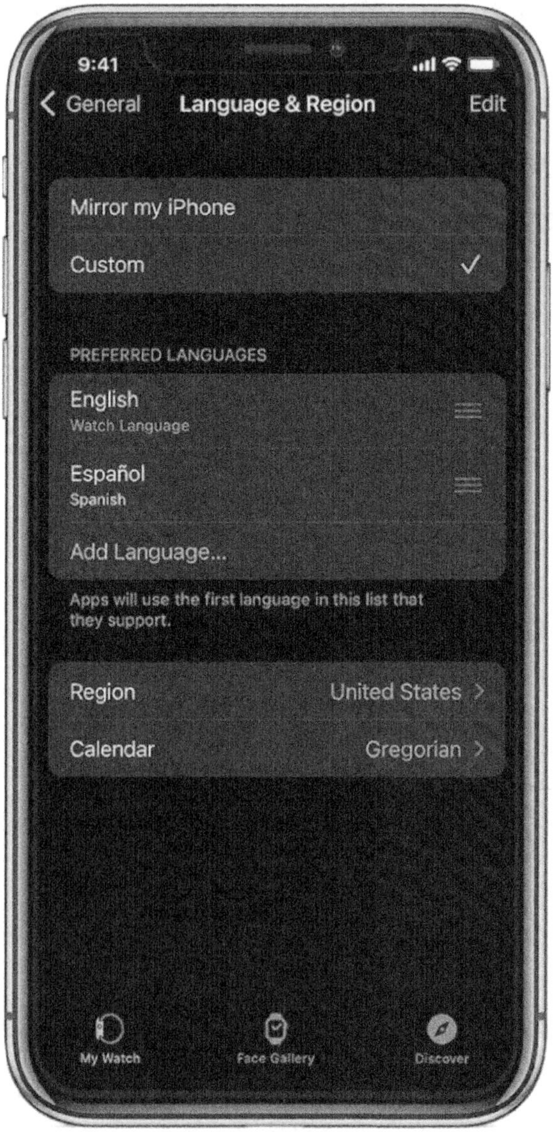

Change wrist or Digital Crown orientation

If you want to use your watch on your other wrist or you would rather have the Digital Crown on the other side, change the orientation setting so that rotating the Digital Crown moves things in the expected direction.

- Enter the Settings application on your smartwatch.
- Head over to General > Orientation.

You can also enter the Watch application on your phone, touch My Watch, and then head over to General > Watch Orientation.

Set an alarm

- Enter the Alarms application.
- Touch the **Add Alarm** button.

- Touch PM or AM, then touch the minutes or hours.
  This step is not necessary when making use of a 24-hour time.

- Rotate the Digital Crown to adjust and then touch the Check icon .
- Touch the Alarm's switch to enable or disable it. Or, touch the alarm time to set snooze & repeat options.

When an alarm sounds, you can touch the Snooze button to give yourself a few minutes before the alarm sounds again. If you do not want this feature, simply enter the Alarms application , touch the alarms from the list, then deactivate Snooze

You can delete an alarm if you don't need an alarm anymore. To do this, enter the Alarms application, touch the alarms from the list, scroll down, then touch the **Delete** button

Setup your smartwatch as a nightstand clock with alarm

- ❖ Enter the Settings application on your smartwatch.
- ❖ Touch General
- ❖ Touch Nightstand Mode and then activate Nightstand mode.

When your watch is charging and Nightstand Mode is enabled, it will show the charging status, the date & time, and the time of the alarm you have set.

If you set an alarm, your smartwatch in Nightstand Mode will gently wake you up with a unique sound. When you hear the sound, press the side button to turn off the alarm, or press the Digital Crown for Snooze to give yourself some time to rest.

Split the check & calculate a tip

- Enter the Calculator application on your smartwatch.
- Type the total bill, then touch Tip.

- Rotate the Digital Crown to select a tip percentage.
- Touch the **People** button, then rotate the Digital Crown to insert the number of individuals that want to share the bill.

  Next, you'll see the tip amount, the total bill, and how much each individual has to pay if the bill is split equally.

Take a screenshot of your smartwatch

- Enter the Settings application, touch General, touch Screenshots, and then activate **Enable Screenshots**.
- To take a screenshot, press the Digital Crown and the side button simultaneously.

Screenshots are stored in the Photos application on your phone.

Force restart your watch

If you cannot switch off your watch or if the problem persists, you may have to force restart your watch. Do this only if you are not able to restart your watch.

To force restart, press & hold the side button and the Digital Crown simultaneously for about 10 seconds till you see the Apple logo.

Erase your watch & setting

- ❖ Enter the Settings application on your smartwatch.
- ❖ Touch General > Reset, touch the **Erase All Content & Setting** option, and then insert your passcode.
  If your smartwatch has a cellular plan, you are given 2 options – Erase All & Keep Plan and Erase All.

You can also enter the Watch application on your phone, touch the **My Watch** tab, touch General > Reset, then touch **Erase Apple Watch Contents & Setting**.

If you cannot enter the Settings application on your smartwatch because you have forgotten your passcode, connect your watch to its charger, then long-press the side button till you see the sliders. Long-press the Digital Crown, then touch the **Reset** button.

After the reset is complete and your smartwatch restarts, you'll need to pair it with your iPhone again.

Update your watch software

- Enter the Watch application on your phone
- Touch the **My Watch** tab, touch General > Software Updates, and if there is an update, touch the Download and Install buttons.

Or, enter the Settings application on your smartwatch, then touch General > Software Update.

CUSTOMIZE YOUR WATCH

Show your applications in a list or grid view

Your watch's Home Screen allows you to open any application you want. The home screen can show applications in a list or grid view. Follow these guidelines to select one:

- From your watch face, press the Digital Crown to enter the Home Screen
- Long-press the Home Screen.

- Select List or Grid view.

Launch applications from your Home Screen

- Grid view: Touch the application icon. If you are already on your watch's Home Screen, you can rotate the Digital Crown to launch the application that is in the middle of your screen.

- List view: Rotate the Digital Crown, and then touch an application.

Press the Digital Crown once to go back to your Home Screen from an application, press it once more to go to the watch face (or press the clock icon on your Home Screen in Grid View).

Double-click the Digital Crown to quickly open the last application you used while viewing the watch face or another application.

Launch an application from the Dock

❖ Press your watch's Side button and then rotate the Digital Crown to scroll through the applications.

❖ Touch an application to open it.

Select the applications that will appear in the Dock

You can decide to display about ten of your favourite applications, or your recently used applications in the Dock.

❖ See your most recently used applications: Enter the Settings application, touch Dock, then touch **Recent**. The most recently used application will appear at the top of the Dock with other applications under it.

- ❖ See your favourite applications: Launch the Apple Watch application on your phone, touch My Watch, then touch Dock. Choose Favourites, touch the **Edit** button, and then touch the Add icon beside the application you want to add to the Dock. Touch the Done button when you have finished selecting the applications.
- ❖ Remove an application from the Dock: Press your watch's Side button, then rotate the Digital Crown to the application you plan to remove. Swipe the application to the left, then touch X.

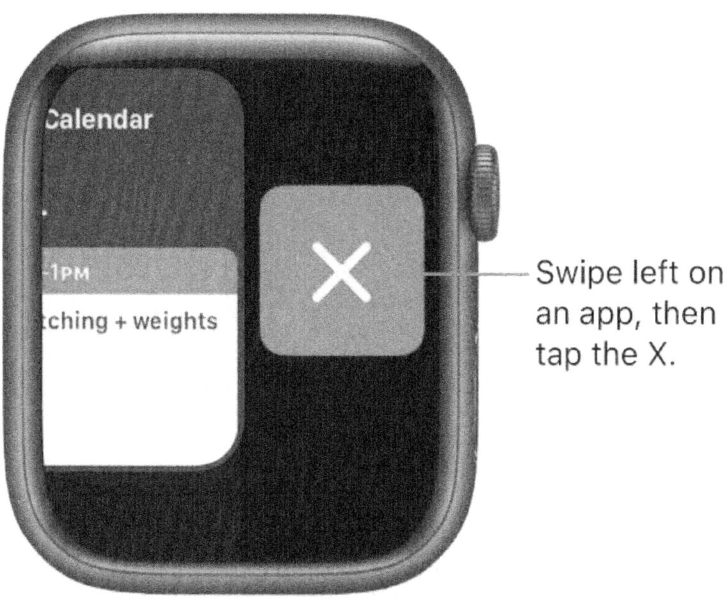

- Go to the Home screen from the Dock: Scroll to the end of the Dock, then touch the **All Apps** button.

Rearrange your applications in grid view

- Press the Digital Crown to enter your Home Screen.
  If your Home Screen is in list view, long-press the Home screen, then touch Grid View.
- Long-press an application, then touch the **Edit App** button.
- Drag the application to another location on your screen.
- When you are done, press the digital crown.

Or, launch the Watch application on your phone, touch the **My Watch** button, touch the **Apps View** button, and then touch Arrangements. Long press an application icon. Then drag the application to another location on your screen.

Note: In the List view, your watch applications are always sorted alphabetically.

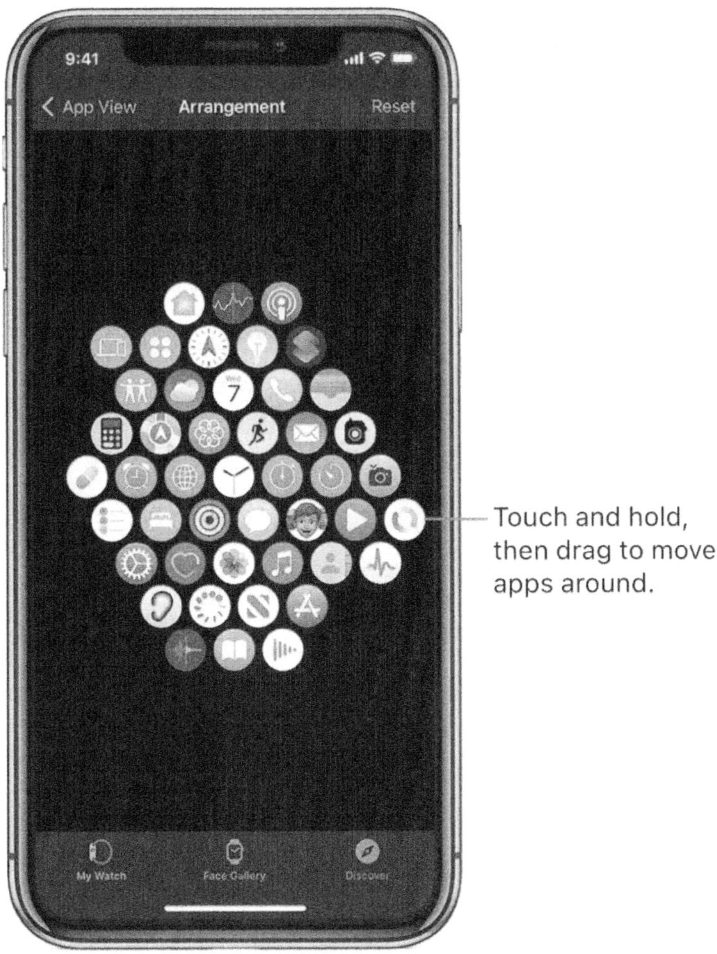

Remove an application from your watch

In grid view, long-press your watch's Home screen, touch the **Edit App** button, then touch the **X** icon to remove the application from your watch.

In list view, swipe an application to the left and then touch the Trash icon to delete the application from your watch.

Note: Not all applications can be uninstalled from your smartwatch.

Change application settings

- Launch the Watch application on your phone.
- Touch the **My Watch** button and then scroll down to check out your installed applications.
- Touch an application to change its setting.

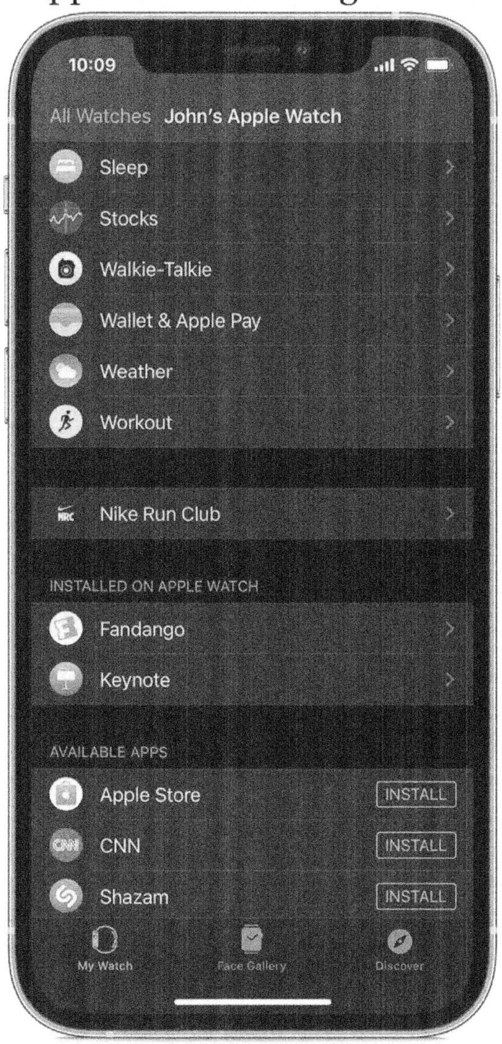

See how much storage your apps are using

See how storage space is being used on your watch—the total used storage, how much is left, and how much storage each application is using.

- ❖ Enter the Settings application on your watch.
- ❖ Head over to General > Storage.

Or, launch the Watch application on your phone, touch My Watch, and then head over to General > Storages.

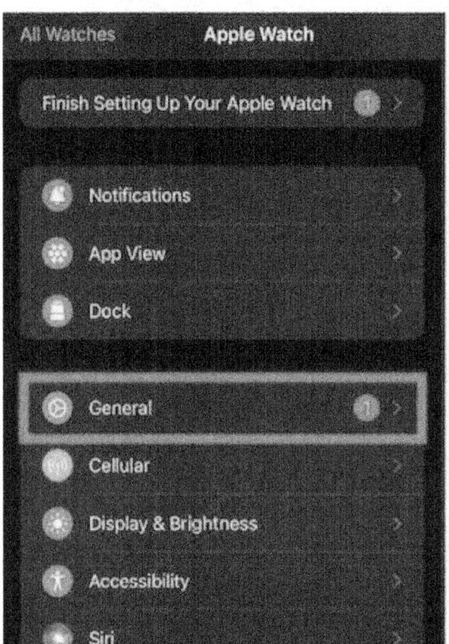

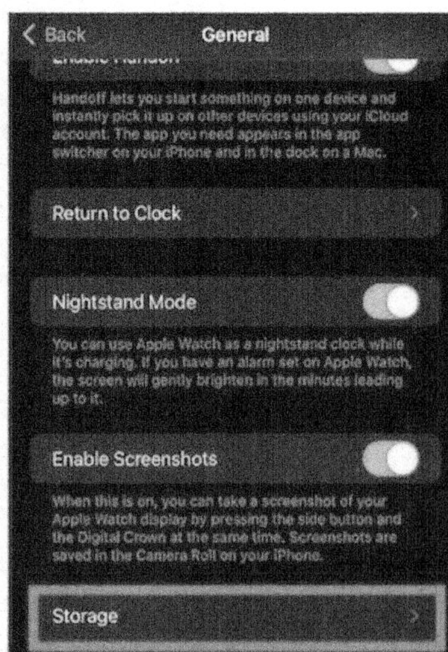

Get applications from the Application Store on your watch

You can install applications from the Application Store.

- ❖ Launch the Application Store app on your smartwatch.
- ❖ Rotate the Digital Crown to check out featured applications.
  Touch a category or touch the **See All** button under a collection to view more applications.
- ❖ Touch the **Get** button to get a free application. touch the price of an application to but it.

If you see a Download button instead of the price, it means that you have already purchased the application and can download it for free.

To look for a specific application, touch the Search bar at the upper part of your screen, then type or dictate the name of the application. You can also check out trending applications categories by touching a category.

Install applications that are already on your iPhone

Applications on your iPhone that have watchOS versions are installed automatically and can be found on your watch's Home Screen. But if you don't like this feature, you can turn it off, and only install the applications you want.

- Enter the Watch application on your phone.
- Touch the **My Watch** button, touch the **General** button and then deactivate **Automatic App Install**.
- Touch the **My Watch** button and scroll to Available Applications.

- ❖ Touch the **Install** button beside the applications you plan on installing to install it on your watch.

Tell the time on your watch

There're many ways to tell the time with your smartwatch.

- ❖ Lift your wrist: The time will appear on your watch face.
- ❖ Hear the Time: Enter the Settings application on your smartwatch, touch the **Clock** button, then activate Speak Time. Place 2 of your fingers on the watch face to hear the time.

  Your watch can also play chime on the hour. Enter the Settings application on your smartwatch, touch the **Clock** button, then activate Chimes. Touch Sounds to pick Birds or Bells.
- ❖ Feel the time: Your watch can tap out the time on your wrist when it's in silent mode, to activate this feature, simply enter the Settings application on your smartwatch, touch the

Clock button, touch Taptic Time, activate Taptic Time, then pick an option.

❖ Make use of Siri: Lift your hand and say "What time is it?"

Control Center

The Control Centre provides access to Apple Watch features like Focus, Theater mode, Airplane mode, etc.

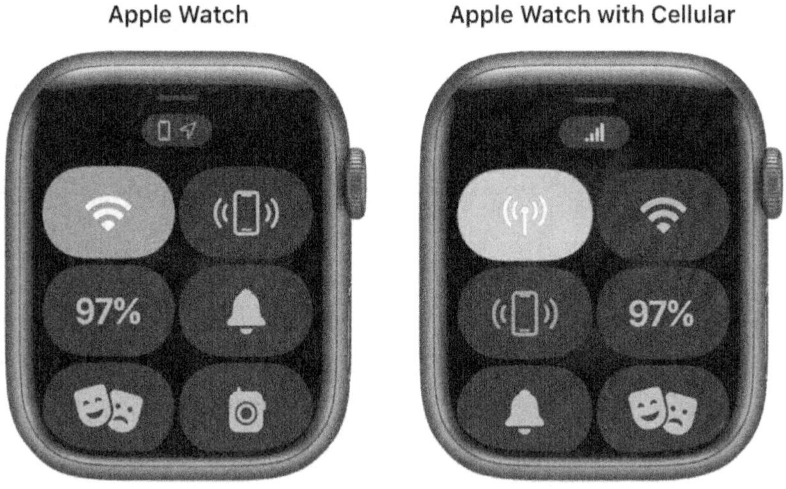

Touch and hold the bottom, then swipe up to open Control Center.

❖ Open Control Centre: Swipe up from the watch face. From any other screen, long-press the bottom of your watch screen, then swipe up.

Note: You cannot open the Controls Centre from your watch's Home Screen. Instead, return to the watch face or launch an application then open the Controls Centre.

❖ Press the Digital Crown to close the Control Centre.

Reorganize the Controls Centre

Adhere to the directives below to rearrange the icons in the Controls Centre:

❖ Long-press the bottom of your watch screen, then swipe up to reveal the Controls Centre

❖ Scroll to the end of the Controls Centre, then touch the **Edit** button

❖ Long-press an icon and then move it to another location by dragging it there.
❖ Touch the **Done** button when you are done.

Remove Control Centre icons

Adhere to the directives below to remove the icons in the Controls Centre:

❖ Long-press the bottom of your watch's screen, then swipe up to reveal the Controls Centre
❖ Scroll to the end of the Controls Centre, then touch the **Edit** button

❖ Touch the Delete icon in the corner of the icon you plan to remove from the Control Centre.

❖ Touch the **Done** button or press the Digital Crown when you are done.

To restore an icon you have removed, open the Controls Centre, touch the **Edit** button, and then touch the Add button in the corner of the icon you want to add to the Controls Centre. Touch the **Done** button or press the Digital Crown when you are done.

Activate airplane mode

Activating Airplane Mode disables WiFi & cellular but leaves Bluetooth turned on.

Long-press the bottom of your watch's screen, swipe up to reveal the Controls Centre, then touch the Airplane Mode button  to activate Airplane mode.

Touch the Airplane Mode button  once more to deactivate Airplane mode

Use your watch's flashlight

Use your watch's flashlight to illuminate objects close to you.

- ❖ Turn on your watch's flash-light: Long-press the bottom of your watch's screen, swipe up to reveal the Controls Centre, then touch the Flashlight button . Swipe to the left to select a mode—steady red light, steady white light flashing white light.
- ❖ Press the side button or the Digital Crown to turn off the flashlight.

Theater mode

Theater mode stops your screen from turning on when you raise your hand. It also activates silent mode.

Long-press the bottom of your watch's screen, swipe up to reveal the Controls Centre, touch the Theater Mode button , then touch Theater Mode

When you activate theater mode, the theater status icon will appear at the top of your screen.

To wake your smartwatch when theater mode is active, simply press the side button or Digital

Crown, tap your screen, or rotate the Digital Crown.

Turn on silent mode

Long-press the bottom of your watch's screen, swipe up to reveal the Controls Centre, then touch the Silent button 

Or, launch the Watch application on your phone, touch the **My Watch** button, touch Sound & Haptic, then activate silent mode.

Find your iPhone

Your smartwatch can help you locate your iPhone if it's far away.

Long-press the bottom of your watch's screen, swipe up to reveal the Controls Centre, then touch the Ping iPhone button

Your phone will play a sound to make it easy for you to find it

Tip: If you are in a dark place, long-press the Ping iPhone button to make your iPhone flash while playing the sound.

Change your watch brightness level & text size

Enter the Settings application on your watch, then touch Display & Brightness to change the following:

- Brightness: Touch the Brightness control to change the brightness level, or touch the slider, and then rotate the Digital Crown.

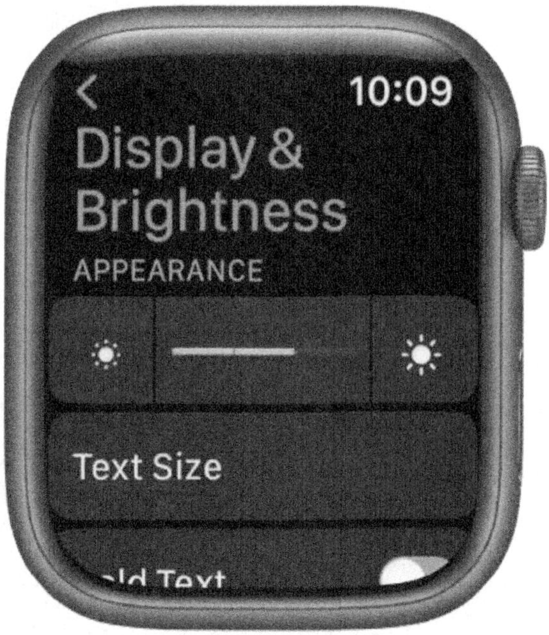

- ❖ Text size: Touch the **Text Size** button, then touch the letters or rotate the Digital Crown.
- ❖ Bold text: Enable Bold Text.

You can also change these settings on your phone. Enter the Watch application on your phone, touch the **My Watch** button, touch Display & Brightness, then change the brightness level & text size

Adjust the volume

- ❖ Enter the Settings application on your watch.

- Touch **Sounds and Haptic**.
- Touch the volume controls in the Alert Volume section, or touch the slider, and then rotate the Digital crown to change the volume level.

Or, launch the Watch application on your phone, touch **Sound & Haptic**, and then slide the Alert Volume slider.

Change the haptic intensity

You can change the haptics strength—or wrist taps—your smartwatch uses for alerts & notifications.

- Enter the Settings application on your watch.
- Touch Sounds & Haptics, and then activate Haptics Alert.
- Select Prominent or Default.

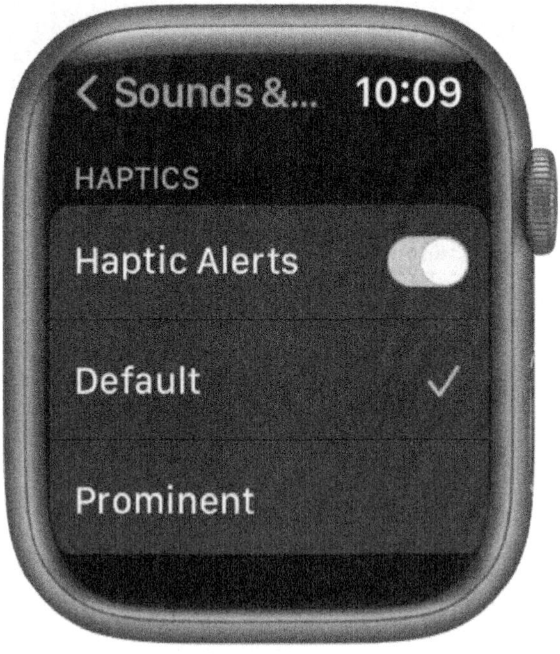

Or, launch the Watch application on your phone, touch the **My Watch** button, touch Sound & Haptics, and then select Prominent or Default.

Activate or disable Digital Crown haptics

You feel clicks when you rotate the Digital Crown to scroll on your smartwatch. To activate or deactivate this haptics, follow these instructions:

- Enter the Settings application on your watch.
- Touch the **Sound and Haptics** button, then enable or disable Crown Haptics.
  You can also enable or disable system haptics

Or, launch the Watch application on your phone, touch the **My Watch** button, touch Sound & Haptics, and then activate or deactivate Crown Haptics.

Use Taptic Time

When you put your smartwatch in silent mode, it can tap-out the time on your wrist with a set of unique taps.

- ❖ Enter the Settings application on your watch.
- ❖ Touch the **Clock** button, scroll down and touch Taptic Time.
- ❖ Activate Taptic Time, then select any of the Settings – Morse Code, Terse, or Digits.
  - ➢ Digits: Your smartwatch will long tap your wrist for every ten hours, short tap for every hour that follows, long tap your wrist for every ten minutes, and then short tap for each minute that follows
  - ➢ Terse: Your smartwatch will long tap your wrist for every 5 hours, short tap your wrist for the remaining hours, then long tap your wrist for each quarter hour

➢ Morse code: Your smartwatch will tap each digit of the time on your wrist in Morse code.

You can also setup Taptics Time on your phone. Enter the Watch application on your phone, touch the **My Watch** button, head over to Clock > Taptic Time, and then activate it.

Respond to notifications when they arrive

❖ If you feel or hear an alert, lift your wrist to check it out.
❖ Touch the notification to go through it.

❖ Swipe down on a notification to clear it. Or scroll to the end of the notification, then touch the **Dismiss** button

View your missed notifications

If you do not respond to a notification when your watch receives it, it stays in the Notification Center. You will see a red dot at the upper part of your watch face indicating that you have unread notifications. To view it, follow these steps:

❖ Swipe down from the watch face to reveal the Notifications Centre. From any other screen, long-press the top of your screen, then swipe down.

Note: You cannot open the Notifications Centre from your watch's Home Screen. Instead, return to the watch face or launch an application then open the Notifications Centre.

❖ To scroll through the notification list, simply rotate the Digital Crown or swipe down or up.

❖ Touch the notification to go through it or reply to it.

To dismiss a notification without reading it, simply swipe left on the notification and then touch the **X** button. To clear all the notifications, scroll to the top of the Notifications Center, then touch the **Clear All** button.

Silence all notifications on your watch

Long-press the bottom of your watch's screen, swipe up to reveal the Controls Centre, then touch the Silent button

You will still feel a tap when your watch receives a notification. To prevent taps & sounds, adhere to the directives below:

- ❖ Long-press the bottom of your watch's screen, swipe up to reveal the Controls Centre
- ❖ Touch the DND button or the active focus mode.
- ❖ Touch the **Do Not Disturb** button, then select an option – On, On until I leave this location, etc.

Show notifications on your lock screen

You can decide how you want notifications to be displayed on your watch's lock screen.

- ❖ Enter the Settings application on your watch.
- ❖ Touch the **Notifications** button.
- ❖ Pick any of the options below:
  - ➢ Show Summary When Locked.
  - ➢ Touch the view full notification: When you lift your hand to view a notification, you'll see a summary, followed by the full details some seconds later. Activate this option to prevent the full notification from appearing on your lock screen unless you tap it
  - ➢ Show notifications on Wrist down.

Activate Handwashing

Your smartwatch can detect when you start washing your hands and encourages you to continue for 20 seconds, the time recommended by the WHO.

- ❖ Enter the Settings application on your watch.

❖ Touch Handwashing, then activate Handwashing Timer.

When your smartwatch notices that you have started washing your hands, it will start a 20-second timer. If you stop washing your hands in less than 20 seconds, you will be prompted to complete the task.

Get hand-washing alerts

Your smartwatch can remind you to wash your hands when you get home.

❖ Enter the Settings application on your watch.
❖ Touch the **Handwashing** button, then activate Handwashing Reminders.

Connect your watch to Bluetooth speakers or headphones

Play audio from your smartwatch on a Bluetooth speaker or headphone

Adhere to the directives that came with the headset to put it in discovery mode. After doing that, adhere to the directives below:

❖ Enter the Settings application on your watch
❖ Touch Bluetooth.
❖ Touch the name of the device when you see it.

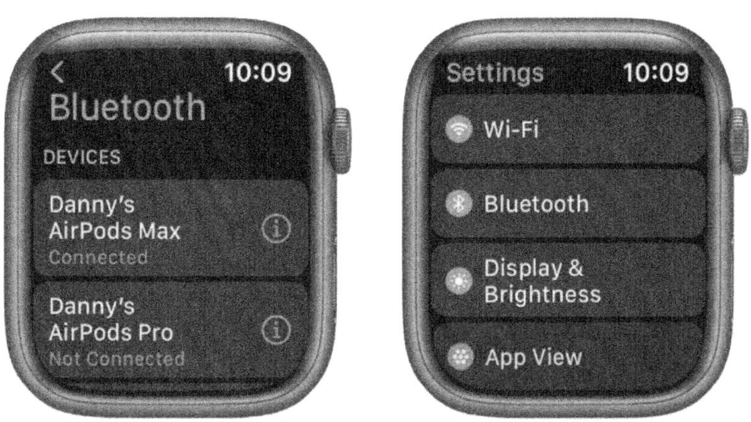

Choose a sound output

- Long-press the bottom of your watch's screen, swipe up to reveal the Controls Centre
- Touch the speaker button , then select the one you want.

Keep track of your headphone volume

- Long-press the bottom of your watch's screen, swipe up to reveal the Controls Centre
- Touch the headphone volume button while listening to your headphone
  A meter will show the current volume of your headphones.

Reduce loud sounds

Your smartwatch can limit your headphone audio loudness to a certain decibel level.

- Enter the Settings application on your watch.
- Touch Sound and Haptics>Headphone Safety, then touch the **Reduce Loud Sound** option.

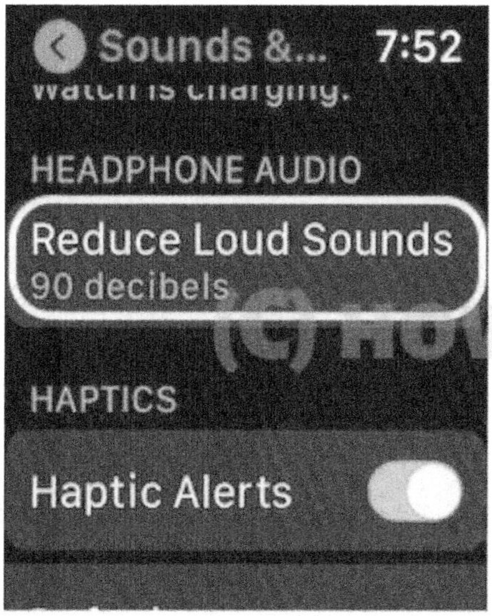

❖ Activate Reduce Loud Sound, then choose a decibel level.

Handoff tasks from your watch

The Handoff feature allows you to switch from one Apple device to another without losing focus on what you are doing. For instance, you can start replying to an e-mail in the Mail application on your watch, and finish replying to the e-mail in the Mail application on your iPhone. Adhere to the directives below to use Handoff.

- Unlock your phone
- Open the Application Switcher on your iPhone
- Touch the button that shows up at the lower part of your display to continue working on the application on your iPhone.

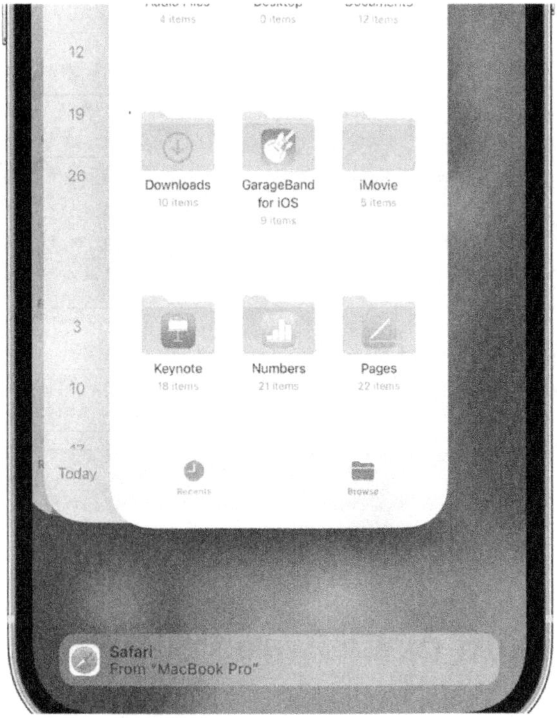

Tip: If you can't find the button in the Application Switcher, ensure you have activated Handoff on your phone in the Settings application> General > AirPlay & Handoff.

To deactivate Hand Off on your watch, launch the Watch application on your phone, touch the **My Watch** button, touch General, and deactivate **Enable Hand-off**.

Unlock your iPhone with your smartwatch

You can unlock your iPhone with your smartwatch if an obstruction is preventing Face ID from recognizing your face.

- On your phone, enter the Settings application, touch Face ID and Passcode, then type your pass-code.
- Scroll to the Unlock With Apple Watch section, then activate the feature for your smartwatch
  If you own more than one smartwatch, you can activate this feature for all of them.

- To unlock your phone, ensure you are putting on your smartwatch, wake your phone, and stare at your phone screen.
  Your smartwatch will tap your wrist to inform you that your phone has been unlocked.

Note: To unlock your phone, your smartwatch has to have a pass-code, be unlocked, on your wrist, and be near your phone.

Use your watch with a cellular network

With a **GPS + Cellular Apple Watch** & a mobile connection to the carrier used by your phone, you can stream podcasts & music, make calls, receive notifications, etc. on your watch even without a WiFi connection.

Add your smartwatch to your cellular plan

Adhere to the directives below to activate cellular service:

- Launch the Watch application on your phone.
- Touch the **My Watch** button, then touch the **Cellular** button.

Adhere to the guidelines to get more information about your carrier's service plan and activate cellular for your watch.

Enable or disable cellular

- ❖ Long-press the bottom of your watch's screen, swipe up to reveal the Controls Centre
- ❖ Touch the Cellular button , then activate or deactivate Cellular.

When your smartwatch is connected to cellular and your phone isn't close by, the Cellular button becomes green.

The Cellular button turns green when you have a connection. The green dots show the signal strength.

The green dots show the signal strength of the cellular connection

Check your mobile data usage

- Enter the Settings application on your watch.
- Touch the **Cellular** button, then scroll down to check out how much data you've used so far.

Setup & check out your Medical ID on your watch

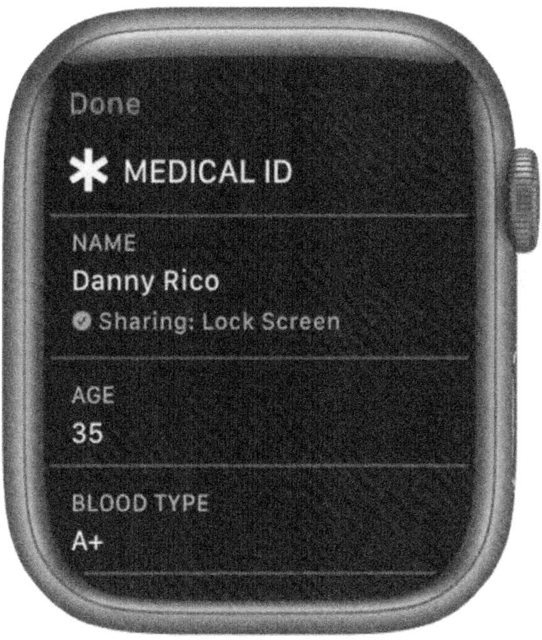

Your Medical ID provides info about you that might be helpful in emergency situations, such as emergency contact info, medical conditions, & your allergies. When you setup your Medical ID in the Health application on your phone, that info is also available on your smartwatch.

To check out your Medical ID on your smartwatch, adhere to the directives below:

❖ Long-press the side button till you see the sliders
❖ Drag the Medical ID's slider to the right side of your screen.

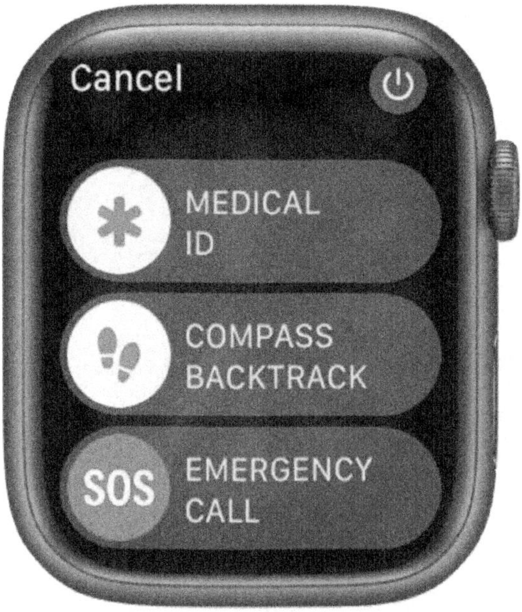

❖ When you are done, touch the **Done** button

Or, enter the Settings application on your watch, and touch SOS > Medical ID.

Use your watch to contact emergency services

In an emergency, use your smartwatch to call for help.

Contact emergency services

Carry out any of the below:

- ❖ Long-press the side button till you see the sliders, then slide the Emergency Call's slider to the right side of your screen.

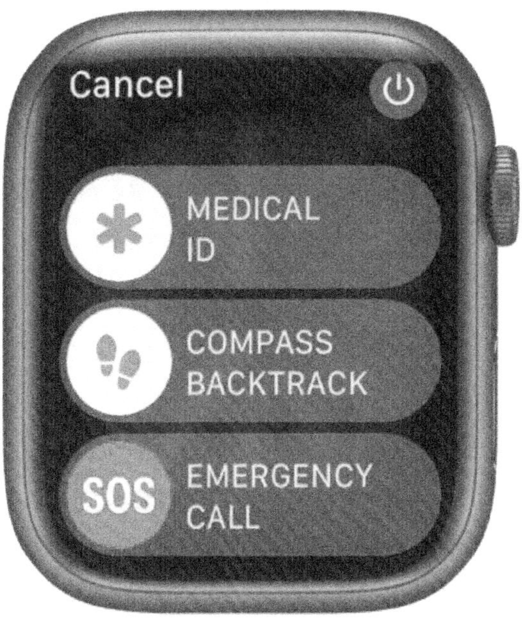

Your smartwatch will call emergency services in your area —for instance, 911 (In some areas, you may have to press a number on the keypad to complete the call.)

- ❖ Long-press the Side button till your smartwatch plays a warning sound & begins a countdown. Your watch will call emergency services after the countdown.
- ❖ You can say "Hey Siri, call 911."

End emergency calls

If you mistakenly start an emergency call, touch the End Call button, and then touch the **End Call** button to cancel.

Change your emergency address

If the emergency services cannot find you, they will go to your emergency address.

- ❖ Enter the Settings application on your phone.
- ❖ Head over to **Phone**, touch Wi-Fi calling, touch the **Update Emergency Address** button, and then change your emergency address.

View & communicate with contacts on your watch

- ❖ Enter the Contacts application on your smartwatch.
- ❖ Rotate the Digital Crown to check out your contacts.

- ❖ Touch a contact, then carry out any of the below:
  - ➢ Touch the Phone button to view the contact's number. Touch a phone number to make a call.

- Touch the Message button to compose a message.
- Touch the Email button to compose an email.
- Touch the Click the Walkie-Talkie button to invite the individual to Walkie-Talkie or start a Walkie-Talkie conversation.

Create a contact

- Enter the Contacts application on your smartwatch.

- Drag down, then touch the **New Contact** button
- Insert the contact's details, which include a phone number, name, e-mail, etc.
- When you're finished, touch the **Done** button

Share, edit, or delete a contact

- Enter the Contacts application on your smartwatch.
- Rotate the Digital Crown to check out your contacts.

❖ Touch a contact, scroll down, then touch the **Share Contact, Delete Contact,** or **Edit** button

Control music, audiobooks, or podcast on your iPhone

The **Now Playing** feature allows you to control audio playback on iPhone & other Apple devices.

To do this:

- Enter the Books, Music, or Podcasts application on your iPhone, then play an audiobook, podcast, or song.
- Launch the Now Playing application on your smartwatch and use the controls to pause, play, etc.
- Rotate the Digital Crown to change the volume level.

If you have more than one Apple device for audio playback—for instance, a HomePod, iPhone, or Apple Watch—the name of the Apple device you're currently controlling will appear in the upper-left corner of your screen.

Touch the < button to check out the Devices list, and then touch a device to manage it.

Stopwatch on Apple Watch

You can use the Stopwatch app to time events with accuracy & ease.

- Enter the Stopwatch application on your smartwatch.

- Select Hybrid, Graph, Digital, and Analog on your screen.
- To use another format while viewing a stopwatch, touch the Back icon< and then select a different format.

Touch the **Start** button or the green button on the analog watch to start timing.

Touch the Lap button or the white button on the analog watch to record a lap.

Touch the Stop button or the red button on the analog watch to record the final time.

After stopping the stopwatch, touch the Reset button or the white button on the analog watch to reset the stopwatch.

The timing will continue even if you launch other applications or go back to the watch face

Analog
10:09
00:00.00
Start or stop the stopwatch.
Record lap times.

Voice memos

Voice Memos
10:09
Recording
10:09 AM
00:32

Use the Voice Memo application to record your personal notes.

- Enter the Voice Memos application.
- Touch the Record button to start recording.
- Touch the Stop Record button to stop recording.

To play a voice memo, enter the Voice Memos application, touch one of your recordings, then touch the Play icon to play the recording. To change the name or delete a recording, touch the More Options icon •••, then touch the **Edit Name** or **Delete** button

Check the weather conditions

❖ Check the current temperature and weather conditions: Enter the Weather application on your smartwatch. Touch a city, then touch the screen to scroll through the hourly predictions of temperature, conditions, or rain.

❖ View a 10-day prediction, humidity, wind speed, visibility, & UV index info: Touch a city, then scroll down.

Touch the Back button< in the upper left part of your screen to go back to the cities list.

Check the time in other cities

- ❖ Enter the Work Clock application
- ❖ Rotate the Digital Crown to scroll through the list.
- ❖ To find more info about a city, which includes sunrise & sunset time, touch the city in the list. When viewing information about a city, you can scroll to find the previous or next city on your list.

❖ When you are done, touch the < button in the upper left corner or swipe right to go back to the list of cities.

To add a city, touch the **Add City** button, type the city name, and touch the name of the city to add the city to World Clock.

To remove a city, swipe left on the city in the list, then touch the Remove button X.

Retrace your steps

You can use the Compass application to track your way and help you retrace your steps if you get lost.

Note: Backtrack is intended for use in remote locations—away from familiar locations such as your workplace or home—and outside densely populated places that don't have WiFi.

❖ Enter the Compass application .

- Touch the Backtrack icon, then touch the **Start** button to start recording your path.
- To retrace your steps, touch the Pause icon, then touch the **Retrace Steps** button.
  The location where you first touch the Backtrack icon will appear on your compass.
- Follow the path to go back to where you first activated the Backtrack feature.
- When you're done, touch the Backtrack icon, and then touch the **Delete Steps** button.

CHANGE YOUR WATCH BAND

First thing is to make sure that you're using a band that matches the size of your watch case.

1. Put the face of your smartwatch down on a clean surface, like a soft, padded mat or a microfiber cloth.
2. If you're using a Link bracelet, press the swift release button to split the band into 2 pieces.
3. Press and hold the release button of the band, then slide your watch's band across to detach it from your watch.

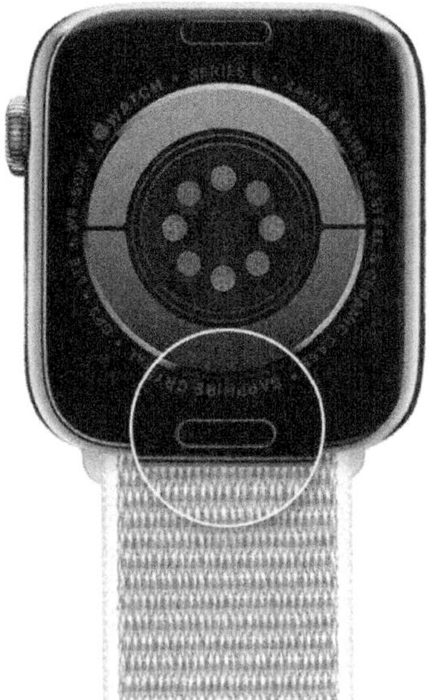

4. If your watch's band does not slide-out, press the release button once more and make sure

you're holding down the button while detaching the band.

5. Ensure the band's text is facing you, and then slide in the new band, don't stop until you hear & feel a click.

Solo Loop or Braided Solo Loop

If you're using a braided Solo Loop or a normal Solo Loop, just drag from the band's bottom to stretch the band over your wrist when putting it on & taking it off.

Milanese Loop

To remove the Milanese loop, simply slide the magnetic closure through the lug or band connector.

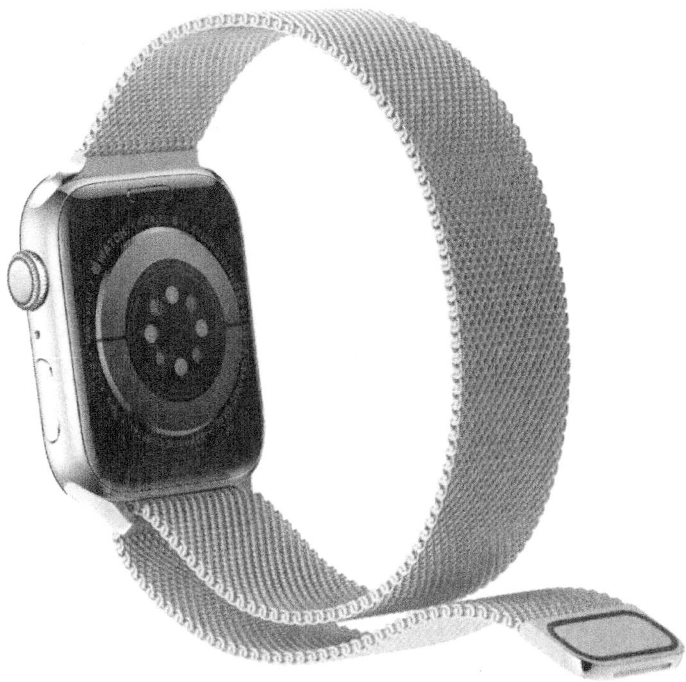

Remove link bracelet

Before removing the watch band, you need to separate the Bracelet into 2 parts. While detaching the band, do not force or twist the band. Adhere to the guidelines below to remove it properly.

Close the butterfly closure

If the butterfly closure is open, fold it one side at a time till you hear & feel a click.

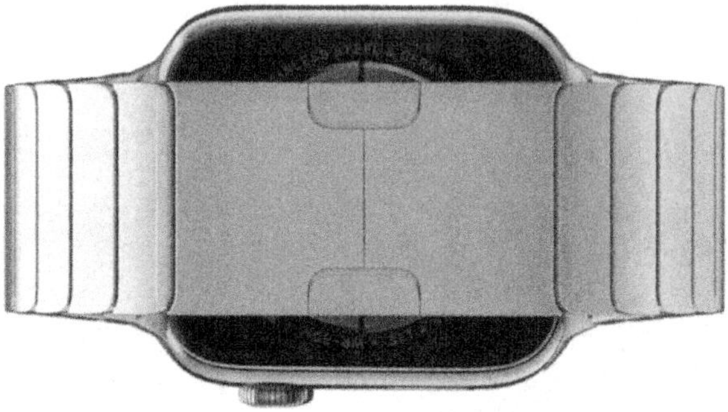

Press and hold the swift release button

The swift release buttons are inside the bracelet. You just have to hold one of the buttons down.

Gently remove the links

Press and hold the swift release button while pulling. Before you remove the band from your watch, make sure you split the band into two parts.

Remove the band

Press and hold the release button of the band, and then slide the band out to detach it.

APPLE WATCH FACES

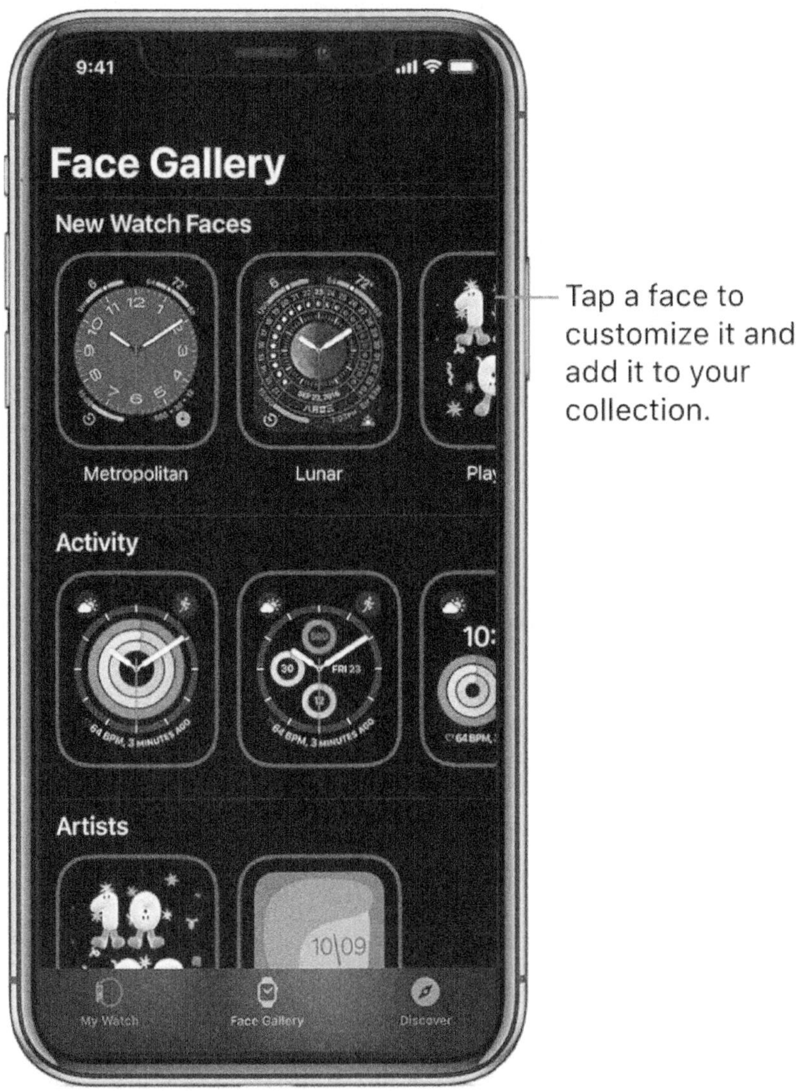

Visit your watch face gallery

The Face Gallery in the Watch application is the simplest way to check out all the watch faces. If there any one you like, you can personalize it, select complications, and add it to your collection.

Open the Face Gallery

Launch the Watch application on your phone, and then touch the **Face Gallery** button.

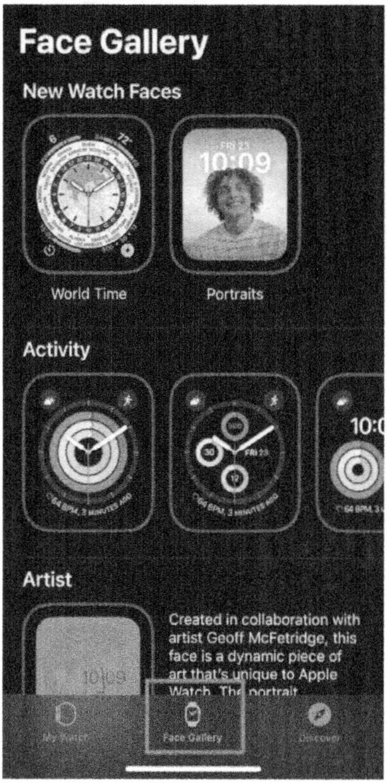

Select features for a watch face

In the Face-Gallery, touch a watch face, then touch any of the features you want (style, colour, etc.)

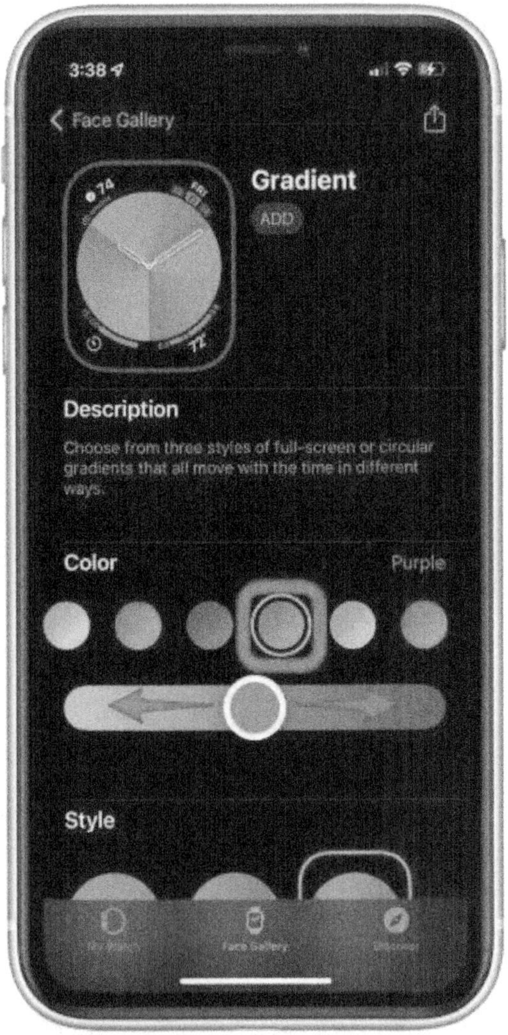

As you try different options, the watch face at the top changes so that you can see the adjustments you have made to the face.

Add a complication in the Gallery

1. Touch a face in the Face Gallery, then touch a complication position, like Bottom, Top Right or Left.

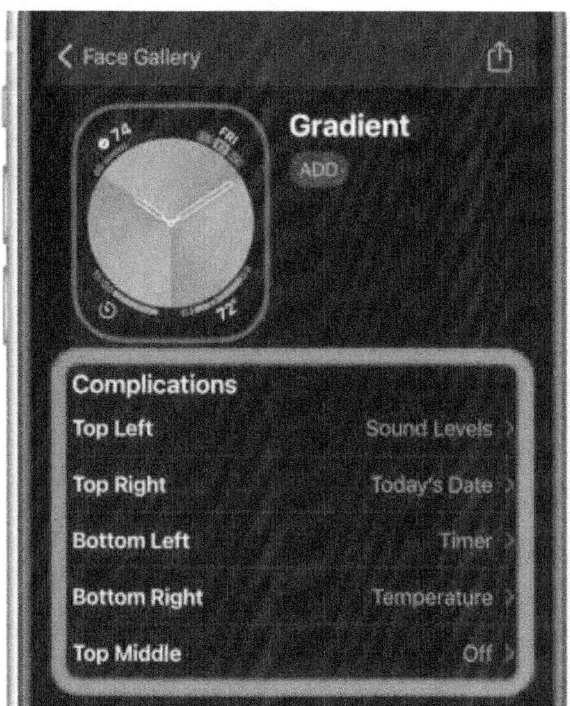

2. Swipe to check out the available complications for that position, then touch any complication you like.

3. If you do not want that position to have a complication, scroll to the beginning of the list and then touch the **Off** button.

Add a face

❖ After customizing a watch face in the Face Gallery, touch the **Add** button.

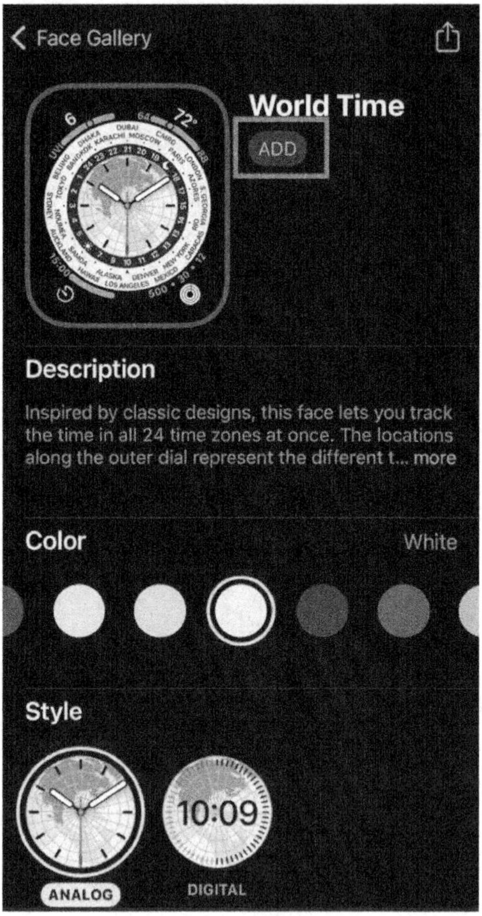

- To move to the watch face on your smartwatch, swipe left across your watch faces till you get to the watch face.

Personalize your watch face

You can customize your watch face to look the way you like & provide the features you need. Select a design, change features & colours, then add the watch face to your collection.

The Face Gallery in the Watch application is the simplest way to check out all the watch faces, personalize the ones you like, and add them to your collection. But if your phone is not nearby, you can personalize the watch face on your smartwatch

Select a different watch face

- Swipe across the watch faces to checkout other faces in your collection.
- To view all your watch faces, long-press the watch face, swipe to one of the watch faces, then touch it.

Add complications to the watch face

You can add features known as complications to some of your watch faces, so you can instantly check the price of a stock, the weather report, and more from your watch face.

- ❖ With the watch face showing, long-press your screen, then touch the **Edit** button.
- ❖ Swipe left till you get to the end.
  If a watch face has complications, you can find them on the last screen.

❖ Touch a complication to choose it, the rotate the Digital Crown to select another one - for Instance Heart-Rate or Home.
❖ When you are done, click the Digital Crown to save the changes you've made, then touch the watch face to move to it.

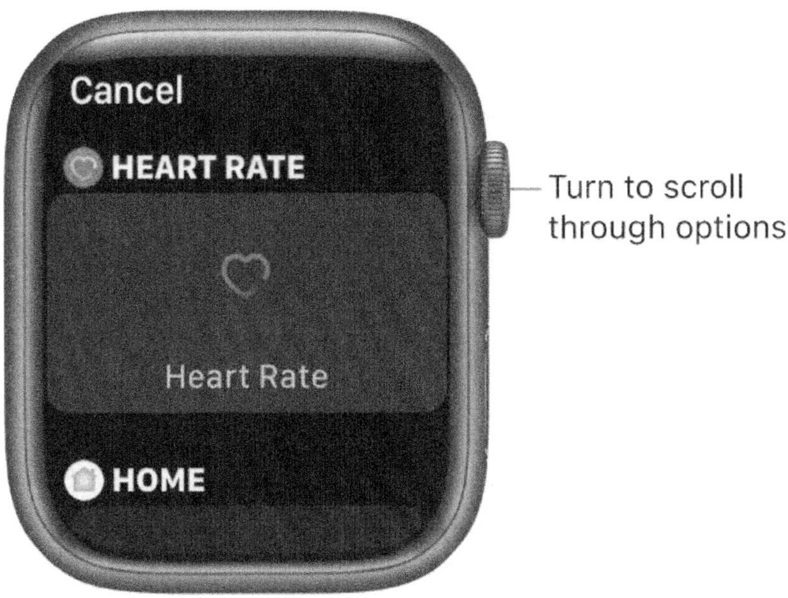

Add a watch face to your collection

Create a collection of custom watch faces, even different versions of a design.

❖ With the watch face showing, long-press your screen.

- Swipe to the left till you get to the end, then touch the Add (+) button.
- Rotate the digital crown to check out the watch-faces, and then touch the **Add** button.

  After adding a watch face, you can now personalize it.

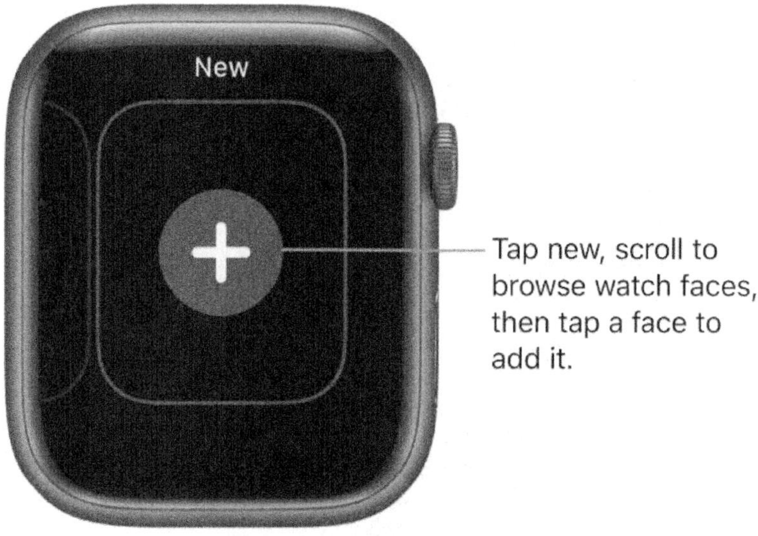

Check out your face collection

- Enter the Watch application on your phone.
- Touch the **My Watch** button, then swipe through the collection in the **My Faces** section

To reorder your watch face collection, touch the **Edit** button, then drag the Reorder icon beside a watch face down or up.

Delete a watch face from your collection

- With a watch face showing, long-press your screen.
- Swipe to the watch face you want to delete, then swipe the watch face up and touch the **Remove** button.

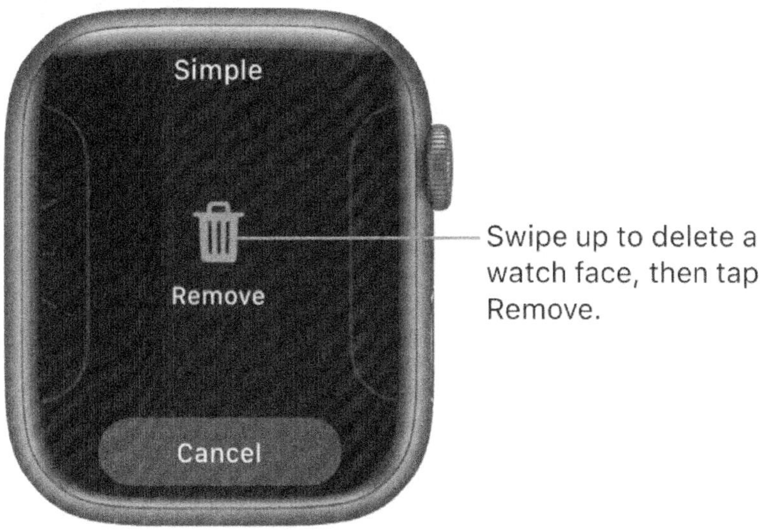

Or, enter the Watch application on your phone, touch the **My Watch** button, and then touch the **Edit** button in the My Faces section. Touch the Delete icon beside a watch face to delete it, then touch the **Remove** button.

Set the watch ahead

❖ Enter the Settings application on your watch.

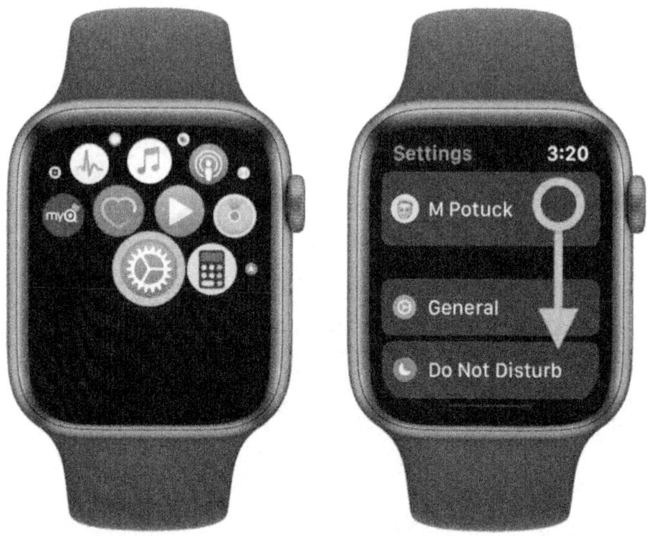

❖ Scroll down, then touch the **Clock** button.

❖ Touch the **+0 min** option, and then rotate the Digital Crown to set the watch ahead.

This setting only changes the time displayed on the watch face - it does not affect alarms, notifications, or other times (like World Clock).

Share Apple Watch faces

You can share your watch faces with loved ones.

❖ Swipe to the watch face you plan to share.

- Long-press your screen, then touch the Share icon.

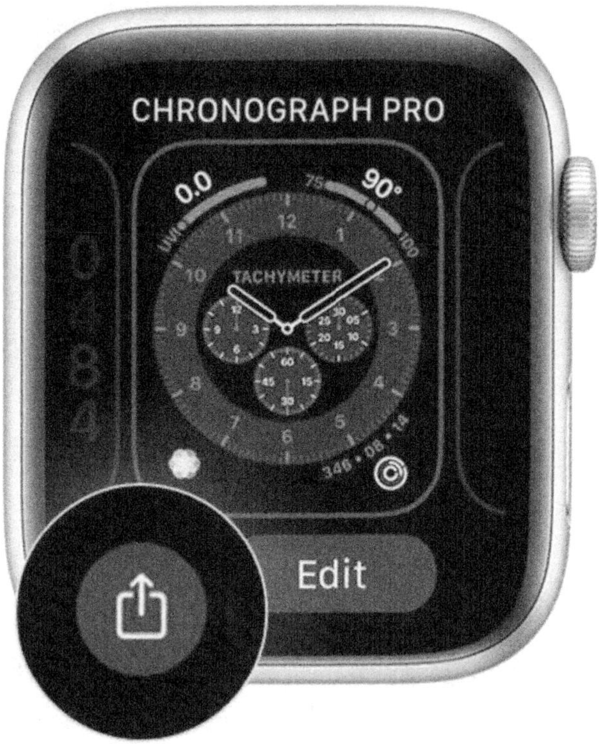

- Touch the watch face's name, then touch the **Don't Include** button for a complication that you do not want to share.
- Touch the recipient, or touch Mail or Message. If you touch Mail or Message, add a contact, subject & message.
- Touch the **Send** button.

Or, launch the Watch application on your phone, touch a watch face from your faces collection or your Face Gallery, touch the Share icon, then pick a method to share it.

Receive a watch face

You can receive watch faces in the Mail or Message app or by touching a link online.

- ❖ Open an e-mail, text, or link that has the shared watch face in it.
- ❖ Touch the shared watch face, then touch the **Add** button.

Create a photo watch face

While checking out a picture in the Photos application on your smartwatch, touch the Share icon, scroll down, then touch the **Create Face** button.

FOCUS

The Focus feature can help you focus when you want to concentrate on a task. It can lessen distractions and let other applications & people know that you are busy.

You can pick from the available Focus modes or create one for yourself on your iPhone.

Note: If you want to share your Focus settings with all the Apple devices signed in with your Apple ID, enter the Settings application on your phone, touch the **Focus** button, and then activate **Share Across Devices**.

Activate or deactivate

- Long-press the bottom of your watch's screen, swipe up to reveal the Controls Centre
- Long-press the DND button or the current Focus button.

❖ Touch a Focus mode.

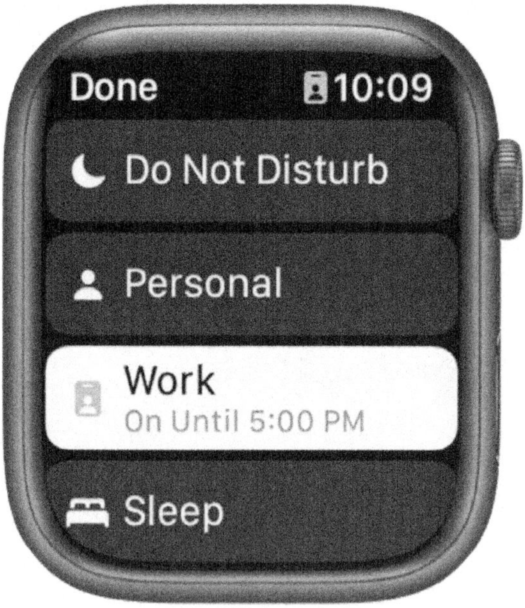

❖ Choose an option - On, for an hour, On until I leave this location, etc.

Touch an active Focus button in the Controls Center to deactivate it.

When you activate a Focus mode, its icon will appear at the upper part of the watch face, beside the time in applications, and in the Controls Centre.

Create a Focus mode

- On your phone, enter the Settings application, and touch Focus.

- Touch the Add icon +, select a Focus, and then adhere to the directives on your screen

Select a Focus watch face

You can set a watch face to appear anytime you activate a specific Focus mode. For instance, when you activate the Work Focus mode, your watch can show the Simple watch face.

- On your phone, enter the Settings application, and touch Focus.
- Touch the **Setup** button beside a Focus mode or create a new Focus mode, touch the **Customize Focus** button, and then touch the **Choose** button under the Apple Watch image.
- Choose a watch face, then touch the **Done** button.

Setup a focus schedule

You can schedule when each Focus mode occurs on your Apple Watch. For instance, you can set the Work Focus mode to activate at 8am and end at 12pm, from Monday to Friday. From 12pm to 1pm you may have no Focus. Then, begin the Work Focus mode again from 1pm to 5pm, Monday-Thursday.

1. Enter the Settings application on your watch.

2. Touch the **Focus** button, and then touch a Focus mode,
3. Touch the **Add New** button.

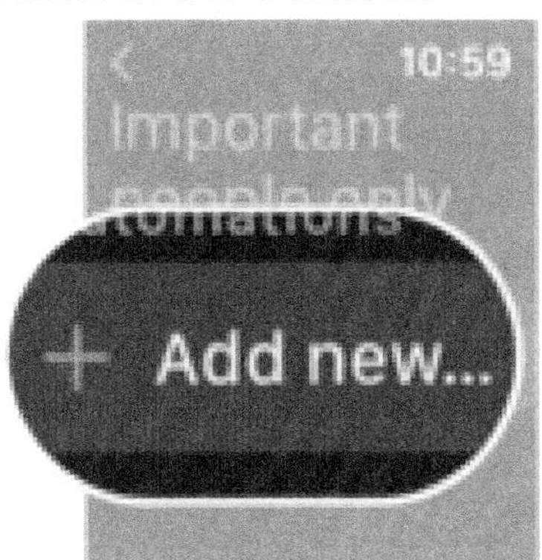

4. Touch the From and To options and insert the when you want the Focus mode to start & end

5. Scroll down the list, then select the days you want the Focus mode to be active.

6. Touch the < button in the upper left corner of your screen to save the options you've set.

Repeat the steps above to add other actions to the Focus mode.

Deactivate or delete a Focus schedule

To delete or deactivate a Focus schedule, carry out one of the below:

1. Deactivate a Focus schedule: Enter the Settings application on your smartwatch, touch the **Focus** button, then touch a Focus mode.
   Touch a schedule, scroll, and then deactivate **Enabled**.
   Activate **Enabled** if you would like the schedule to be activated once more.
2. Delete a Focus schedule: Enter the Settings application on your smartwatch, touch the **Focus** button, then touch a Focus mode.
   Touch a schedule, scroll, and then touch the **Delete** button.

SIRI

With the help of Siri, you can perform tasks & receive answers to your questions on your watch. You can tell Siri to translate a sentence, set an alarm, find a place, etc.

Setup Siri

1. On your paired iPhone, enter the Settings application, touch Siri & Search, then activate Listen for "Hey Siri" and also activate Press Side Button for Siri or Press Home for Siri.

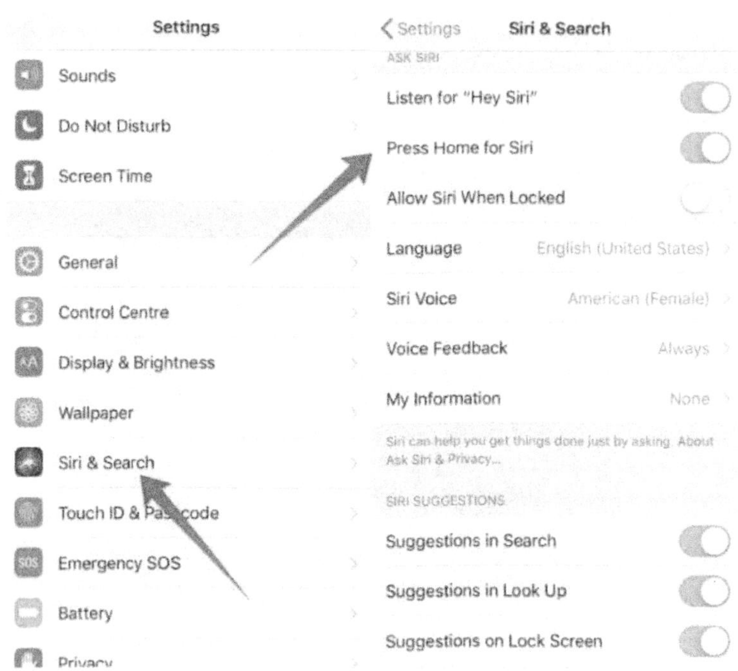

2. On your smartwatch, enter the Settings application, touch Siri, then activate Raise To Speak, Listen for Hey Siri, and Press Digital Crown.

How to use Siri

To request for something, carry out any of the below:

1. Bring your wrist close to your mouth, then speak to your smartwatch.
   To deactivate this feature, enter the Settings application on your watch, touch Siri, and then deactivate **Raise to Speak**.
2. Say "Hey Siri" then ask a question or make a request.

To deactivate this feature, enter the Settings application on your watch, touch Siri, and then deactivate **Listen for Hey Siri**.

3. Long-press the Digital Crown till you see Siri's listening indicator, then say what you want Siri to do for you.

   To deactivate this feature, enter the Settings application on your watch, touch Siri, and then deactivate **Press Digital Crown**

Tip: After summoning Siri, you can put your hands down. You will feel a tap when there is a response.

To continue the conversation or reply to a question from Siri, simply long-press the Digital Crown & talk.

Choose how Siri responds

Enter the Settings application on your watch, touch Siri, touch Siri Response, then select from the below:

- Always on: Siri will speak responses, even when you put your watch in silent mode.
- Control with Silent Mode: Siri will not speak responses when you put your watch in silent mode.
- Headphone only: Siri will only speak responses when you connect your smartwatch to a Bluetooth headphone.

To change the voice & language used by Siri, enter the Settings application, touch the **Siri** button, then touch Siri Voice or Language. After touching Siri Voice, you can pick a different type or voice.

Type to Siri

If you're having trouble speaking, you can write a request to Siri or tell Siri to wait longer for you to finish talking.

- Enter the Settings application, touch Accessibility
- Touch Siri and then activate Type to Siri.
- If you want Siri to give you more time to finish speaking, touch **Longer** or **Longest** in the Siri Pause Time section.

Clear Siri's history

When you make use of Siri, your requests are saved on Apple's servers for 6 months to improve Siri's response to you. You can delete them any time you want.

- Enter the Settings application on your smartwatch.
- Touch the **Siri** button, touch the **Siri History** option, and then touch the **Delete Siri's History** button.

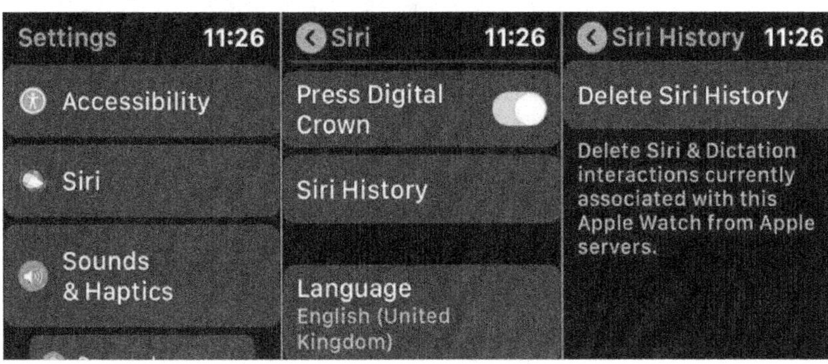

Announce Notifications

Siri can read out notifications from many applications when you are using supported Airpods & headphones.

- ❖ Put your earphones on your ear
- ❖ Connect them to your smartwatch.
- ❖ Enter the Settings application on your smartwatch.
- ❖ Touch Siri > Announce Notifications, then activate Announce Notifications.

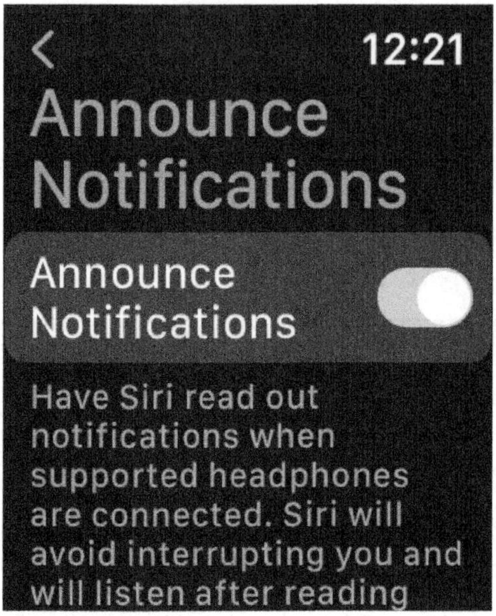

After activating Announce Notifications, you can choose the applications you want audio notifications from by scrolling down and tapping each of them.

Temporarily disable Announce Notifications

- ❖ Long-press the bottom of your watch's screen, then swipe up to reveal the Controls Centre

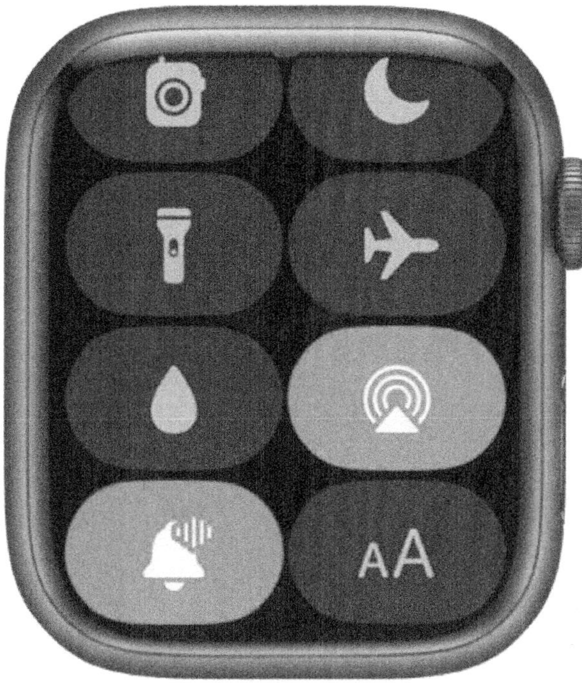

- ❖ Touch the Announce Notifications button .
- ❖ Touch the button once more to activate it.

Reply to messages

Say something like, "Reply, that is good to know."

Siri will repeat the statement you made, then ask for confirmation before it sends your response.

(To send a reply without asking for confirmation, enter the Settings application, touch Siri, touch Announce Notifications, scroll down and then activate **Reply without Confirmations**.)

Stop Siri from reading a notification

Carry out any of the below:

- You can Say "Cancel" or "Stop."
- Press the Digital Crown.

Announce calls with Siri on your smartwatch

With the Announce Calls feature, Siri can identify incoming calls, which you can accept or reject with your voice.

- Enter the Settings application on your watch.
- Touch the **Siri** button and then activate **Announce Calls**.
- If there is a call, the caller is identified and Siri will ask you if you want to take the call. Say "yes" to accept it or "no" to reject it.

FALL DETECTION

With Fall Detection turned on, your smartwatch can connect you to emergency services and send notifications to your emergency contact if it detects a serious fall. If your smartwatch detects a hard fall and you haven't moved for a minute, it will tap your wrist, play a sound, and try to call emergency services.

If the date of birth you entered when you set up your watch (or added in the Health application on your phone) indicates that you are 55 or older,

Fall Detection is automatically activated. If you are between the ages of 18 & 55, you can activate the Fall Definition feature manually by following the directives below:

- ❖ Enter the Settings application on your watch.
- ❖ Touch SOS, touch Fall Detection, and then activate the **Fall Definition** feature.

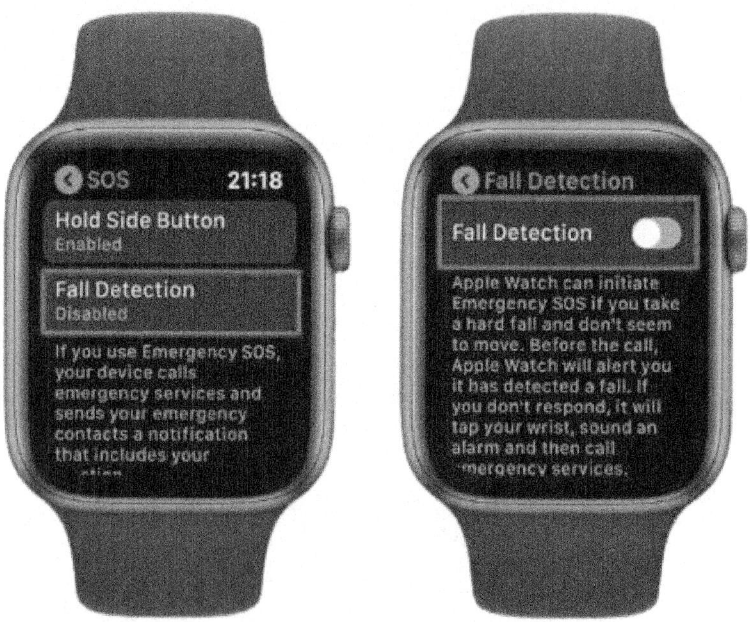

- ❖ Select "Always On" or Only on during Workouts.

How to make a call

Slide the Emergency SOS's slider in the alert to call the emergency department.

How to end a call

- ❖ Touch the End Call icon .
- ❖ Touch the **Yes** button on the End Call display.

What happens if your smartwatch detects that you are inactive

If your smartwatch notices that you haven't moved for a minute, it will begin a 30-second countdown, while tapping your wrist & playing a sound. The sound will get louder so that you & those around can hear it. If you do not want your watch to contact the emergency department, touch the **Cancel** button. When the 30-seconds countdown ends, your smartwatch will automatically contact the emergency department.

When the call is connected, your smartwatch will play a voice message to inform the emergency department that it has detected a hard fall, after that it will share your current location details. If you have previously activated the **Share During Emergency** feature under your Medical ID, your smartwatch will automatically share your Medical ID with the emergency department. The message will keep playing until you touch the **Stop Recorded Message** button or the call comes to an end.

You have to activate Wrist Detection before your smartwatch can automatically call emergency services, To do this simply enter the Settings application on your watch, touch Passcode, then activate Wrist Detection if you haven't already.

Enable or disable fall detection on your iPhone

- Enter the Watch application on your phone, then touch **My Watch**.
- Touch the **Emergency SOS** button.
- Enable or disable Fall Detection. After activating the Fall Detection feature, you can choose **Only on during Workouts** or **Always On**.

Your watch can't detect all falls. It might detect high-impact activities as a fall & activate fall detection.

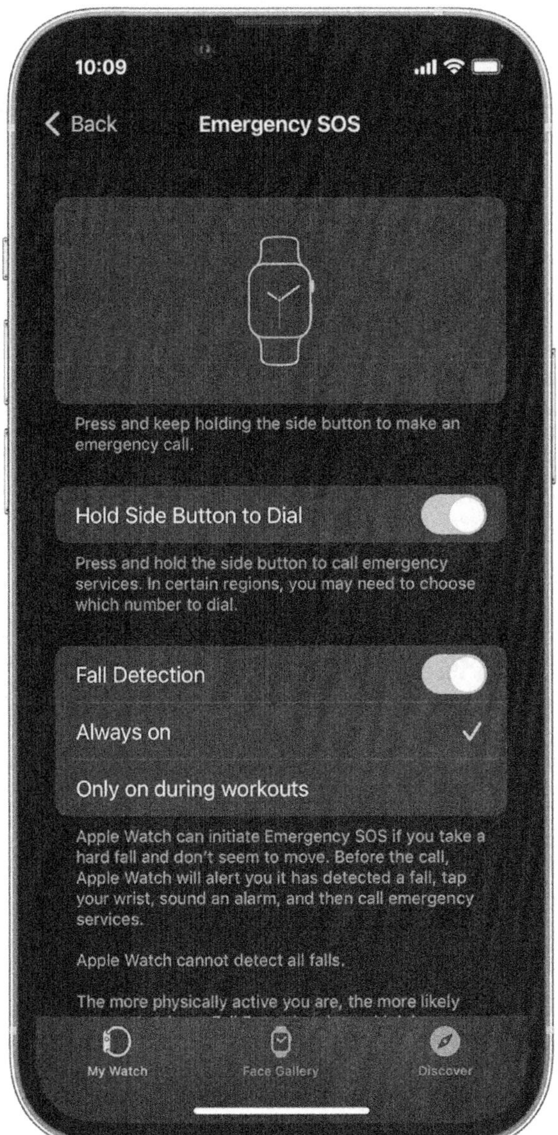

CRASH DETECTION

If your smartwatch detects a serious car accident, it can help you contact emergency services and send notifications to your emergency contacts.

When your smartwatch notices a serious car accident, it will show a notification and automatically start an emergency phone call after twenty seconds unless you cancel it. If you're unresponsive, your smartwatch will play a voice message to inform the emergency department that you have been involved in a serious car accident, after that it will share your current location details with them.

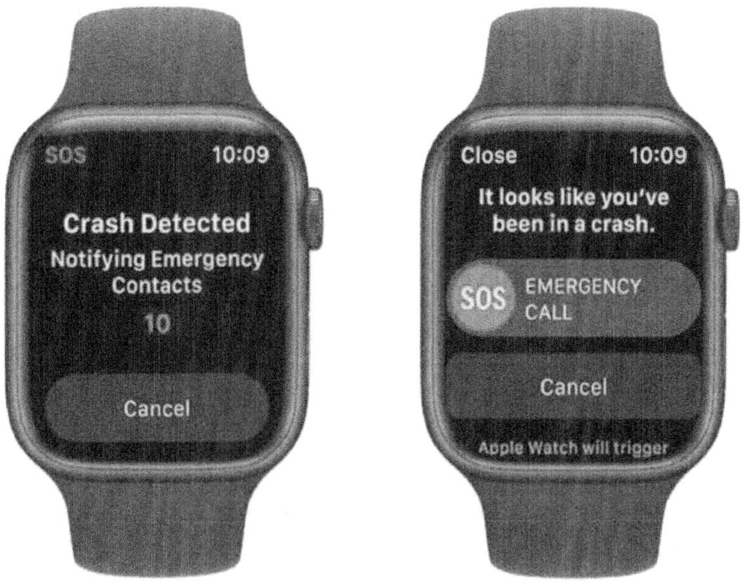

Enable or disable Crash Detection

The Crash Detection feature is enabled by default. To deactivate it, adhere to the directives below:

- Enter the Settings application on your smartwatch.
- Touch SOS, touch Crash Detection, then deactivate **Call After Severe Crash**.

MUSIC

Add music to your smartwatch

You can add music to your smartwatch and listen to them anytime, even when your iPhone is not with you.

Add music using your phone

- ❖ Enter the Watch application on your phone.
- ❖ Tap the **My Watch** tab, then touch the **Music** button.

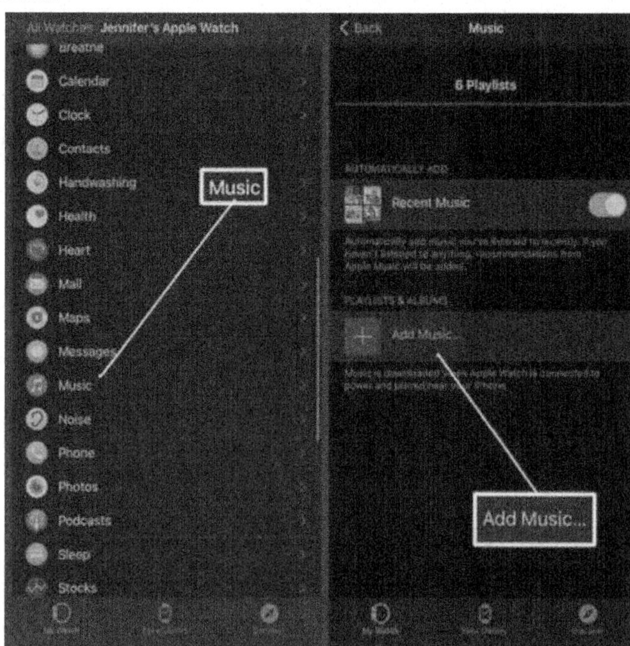

❖ Touch the **Add Music** button under Playlist & Albums.
❖ Choose playlist and albums to synchronize to your watch.

Music will be added when your watch is charging and placed close to your phone.

Add music using your Apple Watch

If you are an Apple Music subscriber, you can add songs with your watch.

❖ Enter the Music application on your smartwatch.

❖ Touch the Search button or the **Listen Now** button, then navigate to the song you want to add.

❖ Touch an album or playlist, touch the More Options icon •••, and then touch the **Add to Library** button.

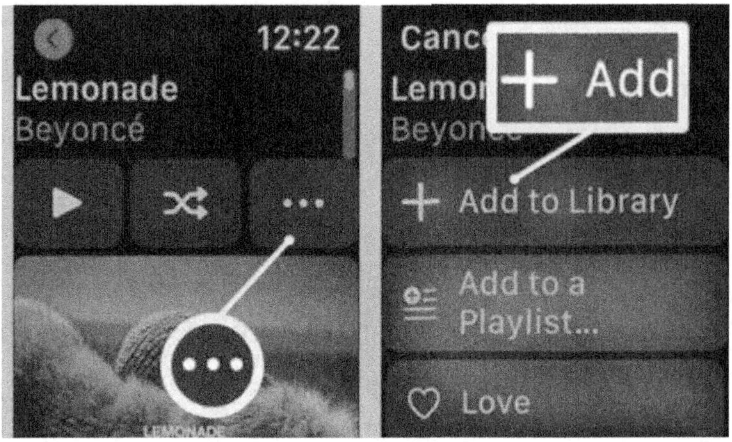

An alert will appear confirming that the song has been added.

Note: You can stream the songs you add to your smartwatch when you're connected to the Internet. If you want to play music offline, you'll need to download it first.

❖ If you want to download the song to your smartwatch, touch the More Options icon ••• once more, then touch the **Download** button.

Music will be added when your watch is charging and connected to a WiFi network.

Add a workout playlist to your smartwatch

You can add a playlist from your songs library that will automatically start playing when you begin a workout in the Workout application.

- ❖ Enter the Watch application on your phone.
- ❖ Touch the **My Watch** tab, then touch the **Workout** button.
- ❖ Touch the **Workout Playlists** button, then select a playlist.

The playlists will be added to My Watch > Music in the Watch application on your phone.

Remove music from Apple Watch

If you run out of space to store songs on your watch, you can remove songs you don't listen to anymore.

Note: To see how much music is saved on your smartwatch, enter the Settings application, touch General, then touch Storage. Or, enter the Watch application on your phone, touch the **My Watch** tab, touch General, then touch Storage.

Remove music using phone

- Enter the Watch application on your phone.
- Touch the **My Watch** tab, touch Music, then carry out any of the below:
  - For the songs you added: Touch the **Edit** button, then touch the Remove icon beside the item you plan to remove.
  - For songs that were automatically added: Disable Recent Music or other auto-added songs.

Songs you remove from your smartwatch will remain on your phone.

Remove music using your smartwatch

If you are an Apple Music subscriber, you can remove songs directly on your smartwatch.

- Enter the Music application on your smartwatch
- Touch Library, scroll, touch Downloaded, and then touch Albums or Playlist.
- Swipe an album or playlist to the left, touch the More Options icon •••, and then touch the **Remove** button.
- Touch the Delete button.

Note: You can also delete individual songs. If you swipe a song to the left, touch the More Options icon •••, touch the **Remove** button, and then touch the **Delete** button, the song will be removed from your smartwatch.

Play music on your watch

After connecting your smartwatch to a Bluetooth speaker or headphone, enter the Music application, then carry out any of the below:

❖ Play songs on your smartwatch: Rotate the Digital Crown to go through album artwork, then touch an album or playlist to play it.

- Play music from iPhone (no Bluetooth pairing needed): Scroll to the top, touch the **On iPhone** button, then touch an album, song, artist, or playlist to play it.
- Play songs from your music library: Touch the **Library** button, then touch an album, song, artist, or playlist. To play songs downloaded to your smartwatch, touch the **Downloaded** button, then select music.

Share songs

If you are an Apple Music subscriber, you can share songs.

- Enter the Music application on your smartwatch.
- Touch the On iPhone, Library, or Listen Now button.
- Touch Songs, Album, or Playlists.
- Swipe left on an album, song, or playlist, touch the More Options icon •••, then touch the Share [Song, Album, Playlists] button
- Select how you want the song to be shared.

WALKIE-TALKIE

Walkie-Talkie is an easy way to communicate with other Apple Watch users. Just like a real walkie-talkie, you press a button to speak and release the button to listen to what the other person has to say. Walkie-Talkie requires both participants to be connected to a WiFi network, iPhone, or cellular connection.

Invite friends to use Walkie-Talkie

❖ Enter the Walkie-Talkie application on your smartwatch.

- Scroll through your contact list, and then touch one of them to send an invitation.

When someone accepts your invitation, you can begin a Walkie-Talkie conversation when the two of you are free.

To add another person, touch the **Add Friends** button on your Walkie-Talkie screen, then select a contact.

Have a Walkie-Talkie conversation

- Enter the Walkie-Talkie application on your smartwatch.
- Touch the name of your friend.
- Long-press the Talk button and speak.

If the friend you're trying to reach have made themselves available, the Walkie-Talkie application will open on their smartwatch and they will hear what you've said.

Rotate the Digital Crown to change the volume level while talking.

Talk with one tap

If you have trouble holding down the Talk button, you can use a single tap to speak.

- Enter the Settings application on your smartwatch.
- Touch the **Accessibility** button, then activate **Tap to Talk** in the Walkie-Talkie section.

After activating this feature, touch to talk, then touch again when you are done talking.

Accept Walkie-Talkie invitations

Touch the **Always Allow** button in the notification that pops-up on your screen when somebody invites you.

Remove contacts

In the Walkie-Talkie application, swipe a contact to the left and then touch the Remove button X.

Make yourself unavailable

- Long-press the bottom of your watch screen, then swipe up to reveal the Controls Center
- Scroll down, and then touch the Walkie-Talkie button .

Or, enter the Walkie-Talkie application, scroll to the top, and then deactivate Walkie-Talkie.

CAMERA REMOTE

If you want to set your phone for a picture and then capture the picture from a distance, you can use your smartwatch to view your iPhone's camera frame and snap the picture. You can also set a shutter time to give yourself enough time to put your hands down and raise your eyes when you are shooting.

For this feature to work, your smartwatch has to be within the standard Bluetooth range of your phone (about 33ft).

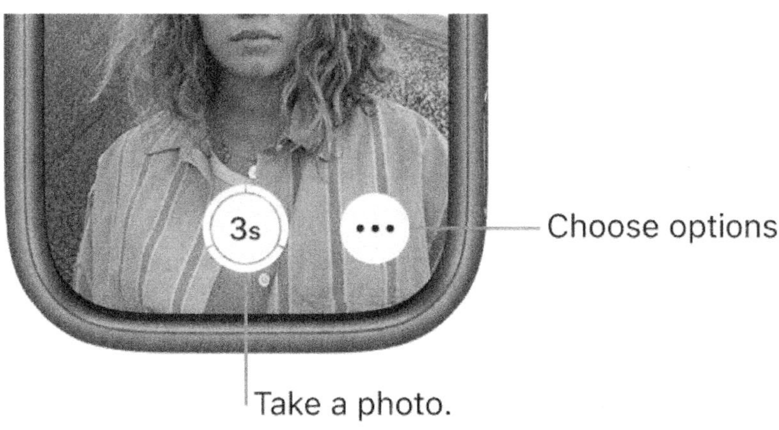

Take pictures

❖ Enter the Camera Remote application  .

- Set your phone to frame the shot with your smartwatch as the view-finder.
- Rotate the Digital Crown to zoom in & out.
- Touch the Shutter to snap the picture.

The picture will be captured in the Photos application on your phone, but you can check it out on your watch.

Review your photos

Use the steps below to review your photos on your Smartwatch.

- Check out a picture: Touch the thumb-nail in the lower left corner of your screen.
- View other pictures: Swipe to the right or left.
- Zoom in or out: Rotate the Digital Crown.
- Tap the picture twice quickly to make it fill your screen.
- Touch your screen to display or hide the shot count & the close button.

When you are done, touch the **Close** button.

Select another camera & change the settings

- Enter the Camera Remote application
- Touch the More Options icon , then select from the following options:
  - HDR (off or on)
  - Live Picture(off, auto, or on)
  - Camera (back or front)
  - Timer (3-sec timer off or on)
  - Flashlight (off, auto, or on)

WORKOUT

The Workout application provides the tools you need to manage your personal workout sessions. You can set goals like time, calories, or distance. Your smartwatch keeps track of your progress and provides a summary of your results.

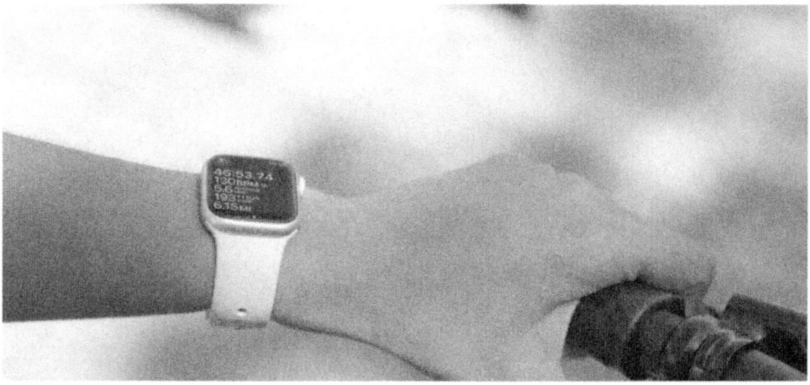

Start a workout

- ❖ Enter the Workout application .
- ❖ Rotate the Digital Crown to the workout you're looking for.

  For workouts like kickboxing or surfing, touch the **Add Workout** button at the bottom of your screen.

❖ When you are ready to start, touch the workout.

Create a target speed for outdoor run exercises

Choose a goal pace for your run outside, and your smartwatch will show you if you are ahead or behind your target.

❖ Enter the Workout application .

- ❖ Rotate the Digital Crown to go to Outdoor Run, then touch the More Options icon •••
- ❖ Touch the **Create Workout** button, then touch the **Pacer** button.
- ❖ Set the distance, for instance, 5miles, then touch Next.
- ❖ Set a time to run that distance, then touch the **Done** button.

  As you run, your smartwatch will display your average pace & current pace, and a graphic will show whether you're ahead or behind the pace you've set.

Your smartwatch remembers your target pace during your workouts. To make changes, select Outdoor Run, touch the More Options icon •••, touch the Edit icon in the Pacer tile, touch Distance• Time, then change the time & distance.

Combine multiple activities in one workout

- Enter the Workout application .
- Start your first workout.
- When you are ready to begin another activity simply swipe to the right, touch the Add icon +, and then select a workout.
- When you're done with all your activities, swipe to the right and then touch the **End** button.
- Rotate the Digital Crown to view a summary of the results.
- Scroll down and touch the **Done** button to store the workout.

Pause, end, or lock your workout

- End workout: Swipe to the right, then touch **End**. Rotate the Digital Crown to view the summary of your results, and then touch the Done button.
- Pause a workout: Swipe to the right, then touch **Pause**. Or, press the Digital Crown & the side button simultaneously. Press the buttons again to continue.
- Lock your screen: it's advisable to lock your screen to prevent accidental taps. To do this, simply swipe to the right, then touch **Lock.** Long press the Digital Crown to unlock the screen.

Track your progress

Raise your hand to see how you are doing while working out. Then, rotate the Digital Crown to check out a different view of the workout.

While walking or running, your smartwatch will tap you every kilometer or mile. If you are cycling, your smartwatch will tap you every 5 kilometers or miles

Personalize a workout

You can add structured intervals to your exercises.

- ❖ Enter the Workout application .
- ❖ Touch the More Options icon beside the exercise you want to start.
- ❖ Scroll, and touch the **Create Workout** button, then touch the **Custom** button.
- ❖ Touch the **Warm -Up** button to set the Target Type or Skip.
- ❖ Touch the **Add** button, then touch the **Recovery** or **Work** button and select a Target Type.
- ❖ Touch the **Cool-Down** button to set a Target Type or Skip.
- ❖ Type your workout's Custom Title.

❖ Touch the **Create Workout** button.

Your personalized workout will appear as a target option for the selected workout.

Change the metrics for each exercise

❖ Enter the Workout application .

❖ Touch the More Options icon beside the exercise you want to start.

❖ Touch the Edit button beside the target .

❖ Touch the **Workout Views** button, then touch the **Edit Views** button.

❖ Touch the **Include** button to add the metric to the Work-out view.

Receive reminders to begin a workout

When your smartwatch detects that you are working out, it will tap your wrist and ask. Touch any of the options on the notification to record the workout, change the type of workout, or dismiss the alert. Regardless of when you tap your screen, you'll get credit for every workout you've done since you started exercising.

To activate or deactivate this feature, enter the Settings application on your smartwatch, touch the **Workout** button, then scroll to Start Workout Reminder.

Receive reminders to end your workout

When your smartwatch detects that you are done working out, it will tap your wrist and ask. Touch the notification to end the workout or pause it, or dismiss the alert and continue working out. If you do not respond to the alert, the workout will continue until you decide to end or pause it.

To activate or deactivate this feature, enter the Settings application on your smartwatch, touch the **Workout** button, then scroll to End Workout Reminder.

Save power while working out

Use the Low Power mode to save battery life during long walks & runs. Your smartwatch will still calculate distance, speed, active calories, etc.

Activate or deactivate Low Power Mode:

- Enter the Watch application on your phone.
- Touch the **My Watch** button, then touch the **Workout** button.
- Enable or disable Low Power Mode.

View your Activities & workout history, and your awards

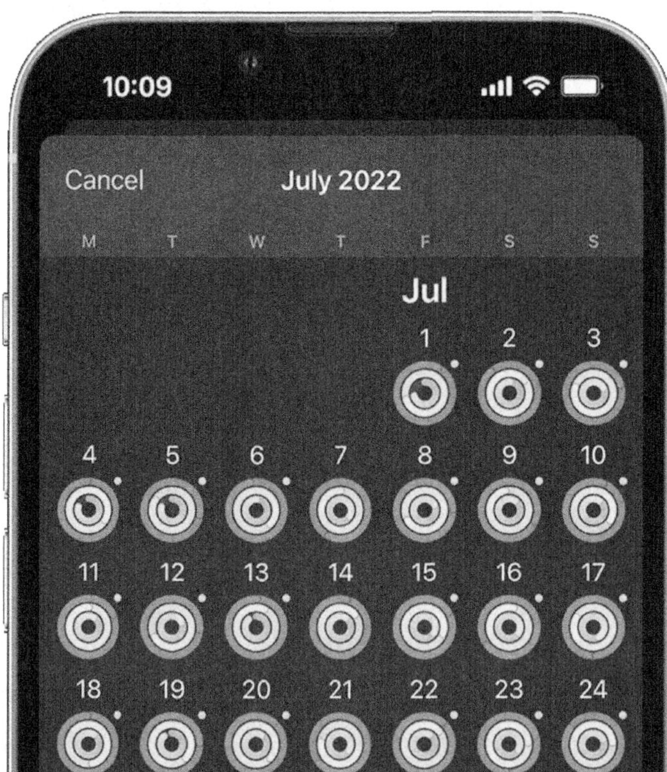

- ❖ Enter the Fitness application on your phone.
- ❖ Touch the Activity progress.
- ❖ Touch the Calendar icon in the top right part of your screen to see your Activity history.

To view your workouts history or your awards, touch the **Summary** button, then touch the **Show More** button beside Awards or Workouts. You can click on an item for more information.

Begin a swimming workout

- ❖ Enter the Workout application .
- ❖ Select Pool Swim or Open Water Swim.

Press the Digital Crown & the side button simultaneously to pause or resume your swimming workout.

When you begin the workout, your smartwatch will automatically lock your screen with the Water Lock feature to prevent accidental taps. When you come out of the water to rest or when you're done exercising, long-press the Digital Crown to unlock your screen & clear any water in your device. You will hear sounds & feel water around your wrist.

See your swim workout summary

Unlock your smartwatch, then touch the **End** button.

The Pool Swimming Workout automatically monitors your sets and when you're resting. Your watch summary shows the type of strokes you've used and the total distance you covered.

Manually clean water after swimming

- Long-press the bottom of your watch screen, then swipe up to reveal the Controls Center and then touch the Water Lock button .
- Long-press the Digital Crown to unlock your screen and clear the water.

Pair your smartwatch with gym equipment

Your smartwatch can pair & synchronize data with compatible cardio equipment like treadmills, indoor bikes, etc. giving you more accurate workout info.

- Check if your watch is compatible with the gym equipment—you will see "Connect to Apple Watch" on the gym equipment.

- Enter the Settings application on your smartwatch, touch the **Workout** button, and then activate the **Detect Gym Equipment** feature.
- Take your smartwatch very close to the contactless reader on the equipment, and make sure the screen is facing the reader.

You will feel a soft tap & hear a beep when your watch pairs with the gym equipment.

If the Detect Gym Equipment feature is off, enter the Workout application, then Take your smartwatch very close to the contactless reader on the equipment, and make sure the screen is facing the reader.

Start & end a workout

Press the Start & Stop button on the gym equipment to begin and end the workout.

After ending a workout, data from the gym equipment will appear in the workout summary in the Activity application.

Update your weight & height data

- Enter the Watch application on your phone.
- Touch the **My Watch** tab, touch Health > Health Details, and then touch the **Edit** button.
- Touch the **Weight** or **Height** button, then make the needed adjustments.

Your smartwatch will use the info you provide about your age, weight, gender, wheelchair status, & height to calculate the number of calories you've burned, how far you've traveled, and other information. The more you work out with the Workout application, the more Apple Watch learns about your fitness level and can more accurately estimate calories burned during aerobic activities.

Pause cycling & running workouts automatically

- Enter the Settings application on your smartwatch.
- Touch the **Workout** button, and then activate Auto-Pause.

Your smartwatch will automatically pause & resume your outdoor cycling and running workouts—for instance, if you stop to cross the road or drink water. You can press the side button & the Digital Crown simultaneously to manually pause the workout.

ACTIVITY

The Activity application tracks your activity throughout the day and prompts you to reach your fitness goals. The application keeps track of how often you stand, how many minutes you exercise, and how much you move. 3 different colored rings summarize your progress. The target is to move more, sit less, and exercise to fill each ring every day.

The Fitness application on your phone records your activity. If you've been active for at least 6 months, it shows daily trend data for active calories, exercise minutes, standing hours, etc. In the Fitness application on your phone, touch the **Summary** button, and then go to Trends to check out how you are doing compared to your usual activity.

Begin

When setting up your smartwatch, you are asked if you want to setup the Activity application. If did not configure it then, you can do it anytime you launch the Activity application for the first time.

- Enter the Activity application on your smartwatch.
- Swipe to the left to go through the Stand, Exercise, & Move descriptions, then touch the **Get Started** button.
- Use the Digital Crown to provide info about your age, weight, gender, wheelchair status, & height
- Select an activity level & walk/move.

Check your progress

Enter the Activity application to see the progress you've made. The application shows 3 rings.

- The blue one show how many times in a day you have stood & moved for at least a minute per hour.
- The green one displays how many minutes you have been exercising.
- The red one shows how many calories you have burned.

Rotate the Digital Crown to view your totals – scroll down to see the progress you've made in graphical form, including your total distance, workouts, total steps, etc.

If a ring overlaps, it means you've passed your goal.

Check your weekly summary

- Enter the Activity application 
- Rotate the Digital Crown to scroll down and then touch the **Weekly Summary** button to see the progress you've made for the week.

Change your goals

If you feel that your goals are too difficult or not challenging enough, you can make adjustments.

- Enter the Activity application
- Rotate the Digital Crown to scroll down, and then touch the **Change Goals** button
- Touch the Minus button or Add button to change the target, then touch the **Next** button.

Every Monday you will be informed of the achievements of the previous week and you can adjust your goals for the following week. Your smartwatch will recommend goals based on your past performance.

View your activity history

- Enter the Fitness application on your phone, and then touch the **Summary** button.
- Touch the Activity area, touch the Calendar icon , and then touch a date.

View your awards

You can get awards for personal records & major milestones. To view the awards, adhere to the directives below:

- Enter the Activity application
- Swipe to the left twice to enter the Awards screen.
- Scroll to view your awards. Touch an award to get more information about it.

Control activity reminders

Reminders can be helpful when it comes to achieving goals. Your smartwatch lets you know if you are catching up or falling behind your performance goals. Adhere to the directives below to choose the alerts & reminders you want to see:

- Enter the Settings application on your smartwatch.
- Touch the **Activity** button, and then set the notifications.

Suspend daily coaching

Adhere to the directives below to disable activity reminders:

- Enter the Settings application on your smartwatch.
- Touch the **Activity** button, and then deactivate the **Daily Coaching** feature

BLOOD OXYGEN

You can use the Blood Oxygen application to measure how much oxygen your red blood cells carry from your lungs to your body. Having knowledge of how much oxygen your blood has can help you understand your overall health & well-being.

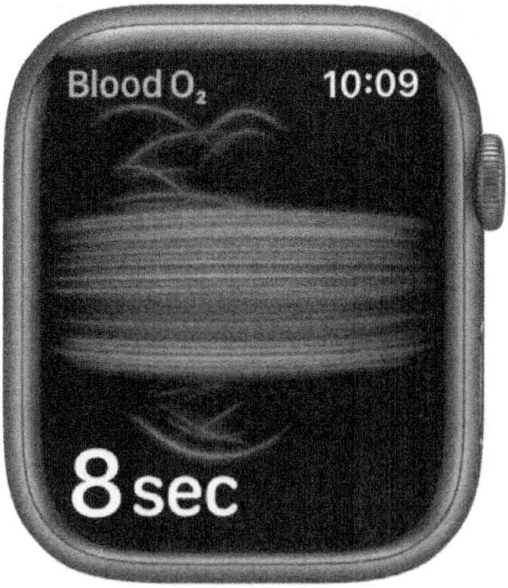

Setup Blood Oxygen

- ❖ Enter the Settings application on your smartwatch.
- ❖ Touch the **Blood Oxygen** button, and then activate **Blood Oxygen Measurement.**

Disable background measurement when theater mode or Sleep Focus is on

Measuring blood oxygen uses a red light that shines on your hand and this light can be more visible in dark places. If you find the light distracting, you can deactivate background measurements.

- ❖ Enter the Settings application on your smartwatch.
- ❖ Touch the **Blood Oxygen** button, and then deactivate **In Sleep Focus** & **In Theater Mode**

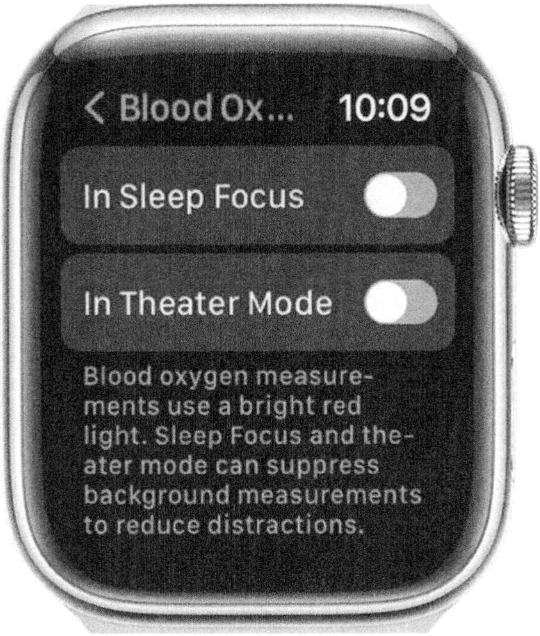

Measure the oxygen level in your blood

The Blood Oxygen application measures the level of your blood oxygen periodically throughout the day if you activated background measurements, but you can take a reading any time you want

- ❖ Enter the Blood Oxygen application on your smartwatch.
- ❖ Place your hand on a table or your lap, and ensure your hand is flat and your smartwatch screen is facing up.

- ❖ Touch the **Start** button and make sure your hand is still for the next 15 seconds.

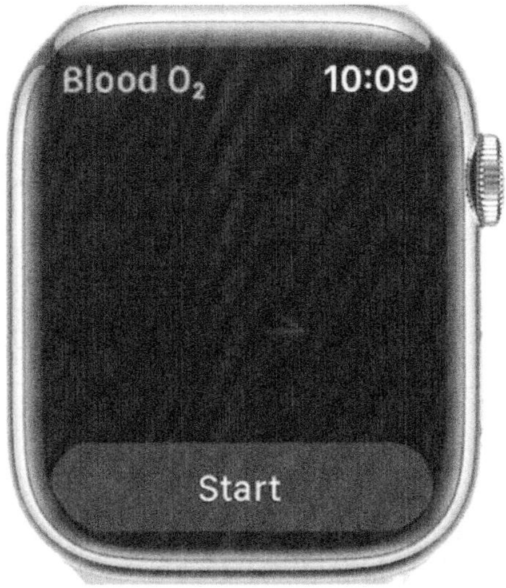

- Once the measurement is complete, you will receive the results. Touch the **Done** button.

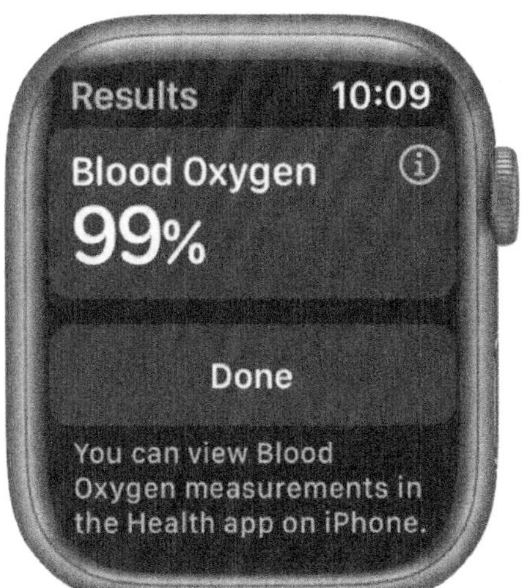

Note: The back of your smartwatch must be in contact with the skin. Make sure your smartwatch is not loose or very tight on your wrist and there should be space for your skin to breathe.

Check out your Blood Oxygen measurement history

- ❖ Enter the Health application on your phone.
- ❖ Touch the **Browse** tab, touch the **Respiratory** button, and then touch Blood Oxygen.

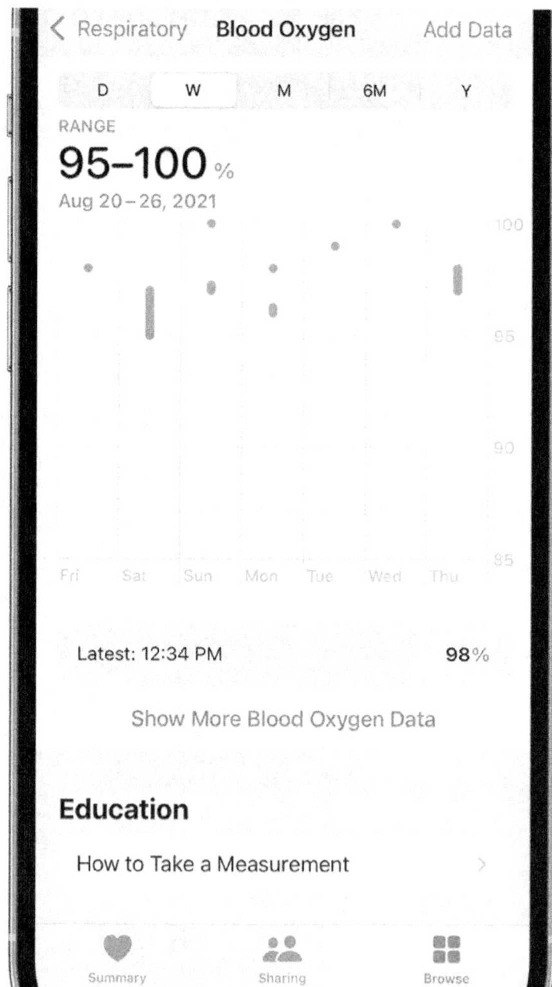

CYCLE TRACKING

Use the Cycle Tracker application to track your menstrual cycle. You can enter flow data and record symptoms like stomachaches or headaches. Using the data you have entered, the Cycle Tracking application can predict when your next period or fertile window will start. In addition to your recorded data, Cycle Tracking can use heart rate data to improve predictions. If you wear your smartwatch to bed every night, the application can use your wrist temperature to improve period prediction and estimate when you're about to ovulate.

Setup Cycle Tracking

- Enter the Health application on your phone.

❖ Touch the "Browse" tab to show the Health Categories screen.
❖ Touch the **Cycle Tracking** button.
❖ Touch the **Get Started** button, then adhere to the directives on your display to set notifications & other options.

To add or remove options after you setup Cycle Tracking, enter the Health application on your phone, touch the **Browse** tab, touch the **Cycle Tracking** button, then touch **Options** beside Cycle Log.

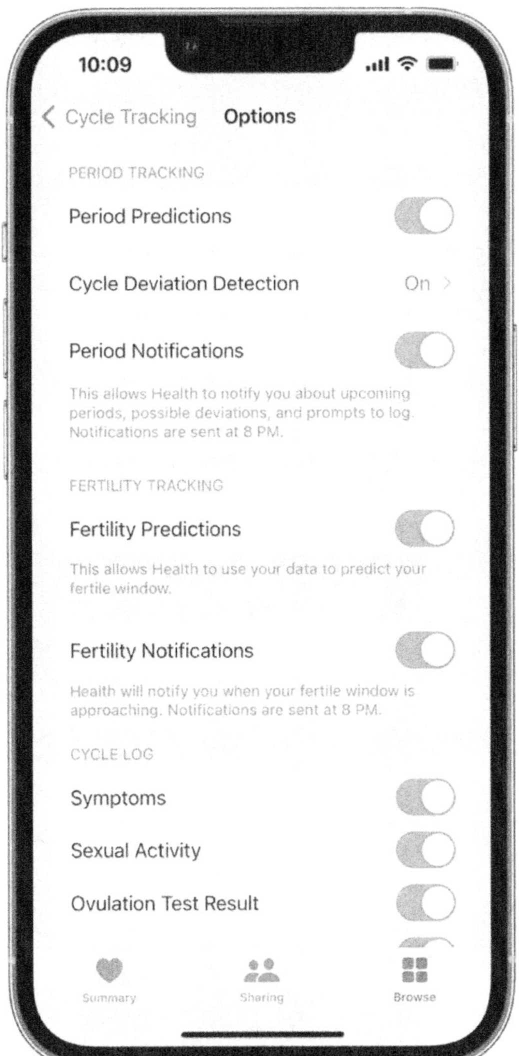

Log your cycle on your smartwatch

- ❖ Enter the Cycle Tracking application on your phone.
- ❖ Touch the buttons & select the options that describe your period - such as your flow rate & symptoms.

The information you provide will show up in the Cycle log on your phone. If you have activated Fertility Notification & Period Notifications in the Health application on your phone, you'll receive alerts about upcoming periods, retrospective ovulation estimates, and fertile window forecasts on your smartwatch.

You can also record factors in the Health application on your phone that may affect your cycle, like contraceptive use, lactation, & pregnancy.

Important: The Cycle Tracker application shouldn't be used as any form of birth control. Information from the Cycle Tracker application shouldn't be used to diagnose medical conditions.

Receive retrospective ovulation estimates

When worn to bed every night, your smartwatch can keep track of temperature changes each night while you sleep and use that info to improve period predictions and provide better ovulation predictions.

Important: The Cycle Tracker application shouldn't be used as any form of birth control. Information from the Cycle Tracker application shouldn't be used to diagnose medical conditions.

Setup wrist temperature tracking

- Setup Sleep Tracking(in the Sleep application) & Cycle Tracking
- To set a temperature profile, make sure Sleep Focus is turned on, then wear your smartwatch while you sleep.
  Wrist temperature info will be available after 5 nights.
- To see wrist temperature info, enter the Health application on your phone, touch the **Browse** tab, touch Body Measurements, and then touch the **Wrist Temperature** button.

The next ovulation prediction should be available after 2 periods of wearing your smartwatch every night.

Note: The temperature of your body fluctuates naturally and may differ from night to night due to several variables. Wrist temperature can also be affected by external factors, such as your sleep environment.

Deactivate wrist temperature for cycle tracking

- Enter the Health application on your phone, touch the **Browse** tab, and then touch the **Cycle Tracking** button.

- Touch the **Options** button, then deactivate the **Use Wrist Temperature** feature.

If you deactivate the Wrist Temperature Tracking feature, you will no longer get retrospective ovulation estimates & wrist temperature info won't be used to predict your period.

ECG

An EKG or ECG (also known as Electrocardiogram) is a test that helps to record the intensity & timing of the electrical signals that cause the heartbeat.

The ECG application uses the electrical heart-sensor on your smartwatch to record your rhythm & heart beat and then checks the recording for AFib (a type of irregular rhythm).

Note: The ECG application is not designed for individuals under the age of 22.

Install & setup the ECG application

The ECG application  will be installed on your smartwatch when you set it up in the Health application. Adhere to the directives below to setup the ECG application:

- Enter the Health application on your phone.
- Adhere to the directives on your screen to setup ECG. If you do not see any setup prompts, touch the **Browse** button, then

touch the **Heart** button> Electrocardiogram (ECG)> Setup ECG App.

❖ After setting up the application , enter the ECG application to take an ECG test.

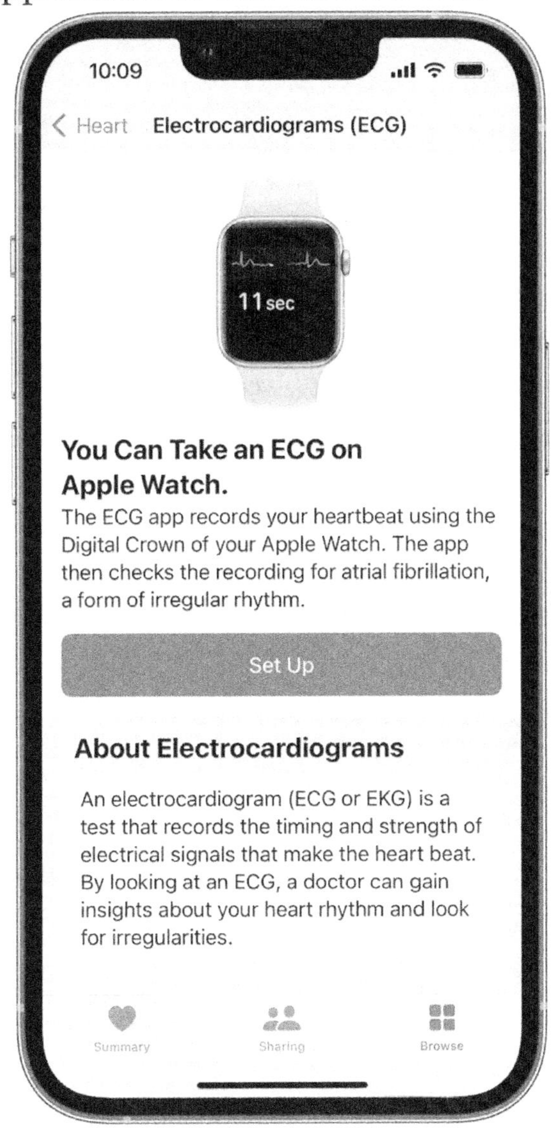

If you still can't find the application on your smartwatch, enter the Watch application on your phone and touch **Heart.** In the ECG segment, touch the **Install** button to install the ECG application.

Take an ECG

- Make sure your smartwatch is not too tight or loose and on the wrist you selected in the Watch application. to check, enter the Watch application on your phone, touch My Watch, then head over to General> Watch Orientation
- Enter the ECG application on your smartwatch
- Place your hand on a table or your lap
- Use one of your fingers to hold the Digital Crown. You do not have to press the Digital Crown while the test is going on
- Wait. The test will take about 30 seconds. You will get a classification at the end of the session, then you can touch the **Add Symptoms** button and select your symptoms.
- Touch the **Save** button to store any symptoms, then touch the **Done** button.

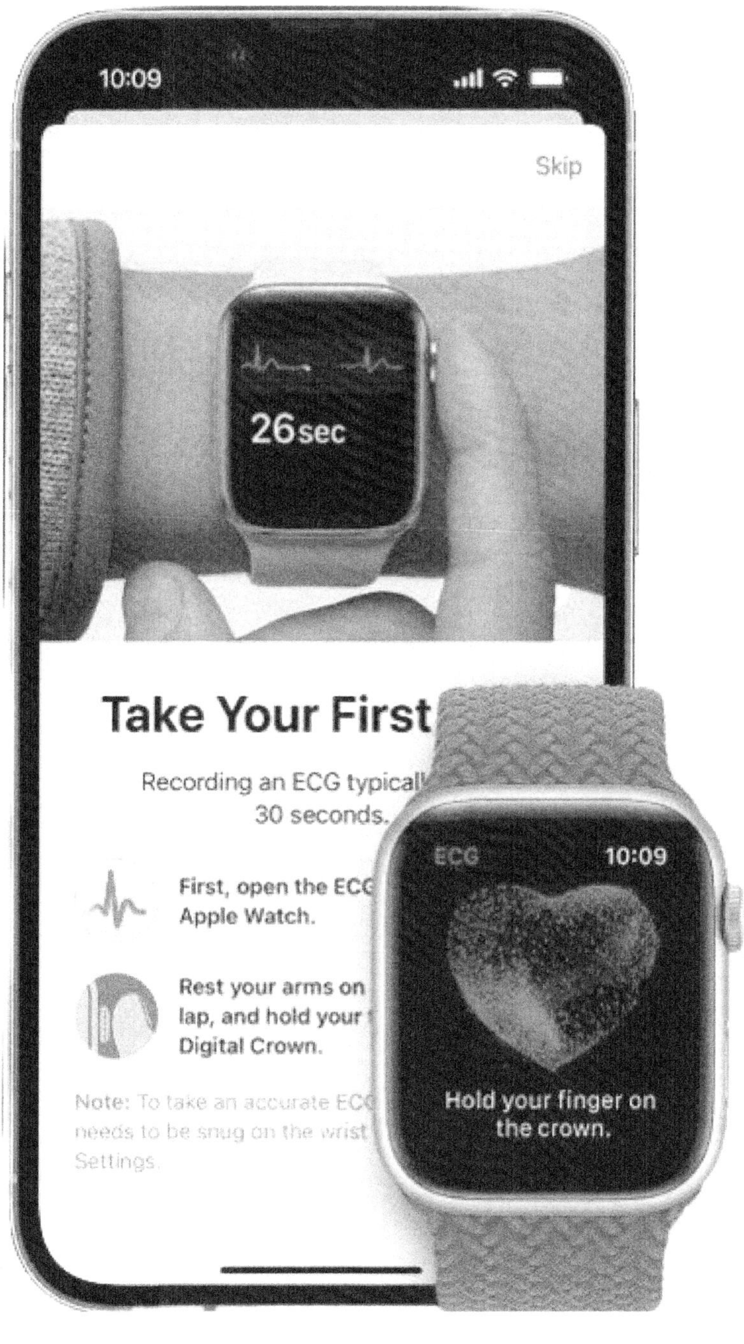
10:09
Skip
26 sec
Take Your First
Recording an ECG typicall
30 seconds.
First, open the ECG
Apple Watch.
Rest your arms on
lap, and hold your
Digital Crown.
ECG
10:09
Hold your finger on
the crown.

How to read the results

After a session, you will get one of the following results on the ECG application. Regardless of what the result says, If you are not feeling well you should see a doctor.

Sinus rhythm

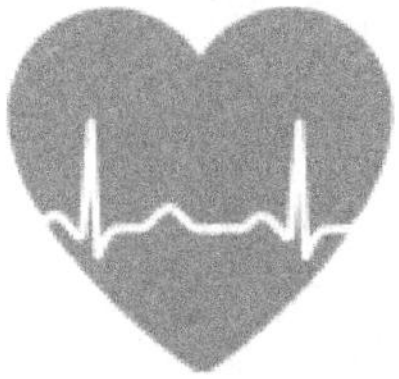

It means that your heart beats in a uniform pattern between 50 & 100BPM.

AFib

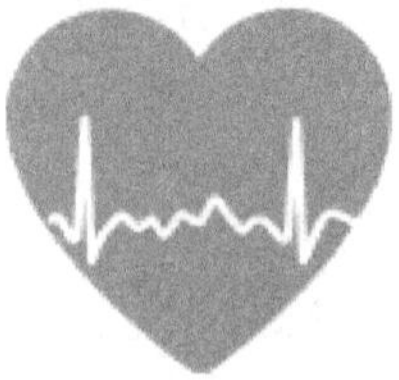

An Atrial fibrillation result implies that your heart is beating abnormally. Atrial fibrillation is a very common form of heart palpitations or arrhythmia.

Low or high heart rate

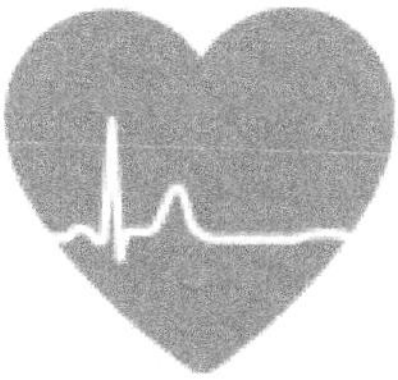

In ECG version 1, a heart-rate that's below 50BPM or above 120BPM can affect the application's ability to check for Atrial Fibrillation. A heart-rate that's below 50BPM or above 150BPM in ECG version 2 affects the application's ability to check for Atrial Fibrillation

- A heart-rate can be high as a result of stress, Atrial fibrillation, infection, dehydration, exercise, alcohol, or other arrhythmias.
- A heart-rate could be low because of some medications or electric signals aren't conducted through the heart properly.

Inconclusive

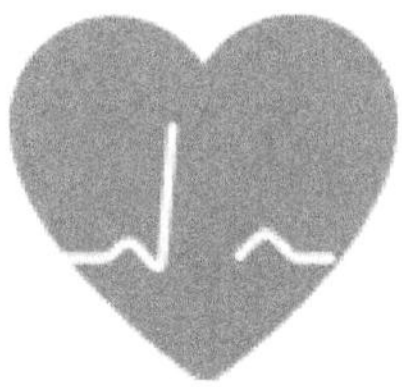

When the result shows inconclusive, it means the recording cannot be classified.

View & share your health info

The ECG Wave form, related classifications, and any noted symptoms will be stored in the Health application on your phone. You can also share the data in PDF format with a doctor.

- Enter the Health application.
- Touch the **Browse** button, then touch Heart> Electrocardiogram (ECG).
- Touch the chart to view your ECGs results.
- Touch the **Export the PDF for your Doctors** option.
- Touch the Share icon  to print or share the file.

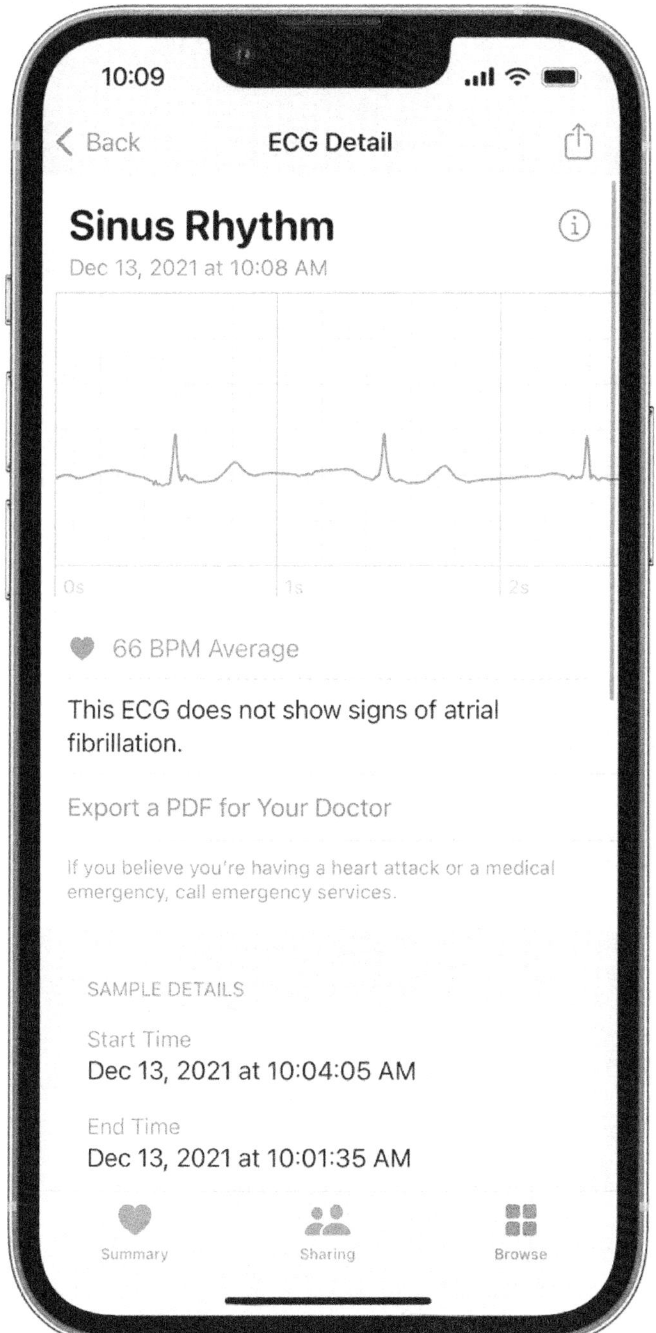
10:09
Back
ECG Detail
Sinus Rhythm
Dec 13, 2021 at 10:08 AM
0s
1s
2s
66 BPM Average
This ECG does not show signs of atrial fibrillation.
Export a PDF for Your Doctor
If you believe you're having a heart attack or a medical emergency, call emergency services.
SAMPLE DETAILS
Start Time
Dec 13, 2021 at 10:04:05 AM
End Time
Dec 13, 2021 at 10:01:35 AM
Summary
Sharing
Browse

HEART RATE

Your heart-rate is a key way to keep track of your body's well-being.

Note: Before you check your heart-rate, ensure your wrist & your smartwatch are dry & clean. Water may lead to poor recordings.

View your heart-rate

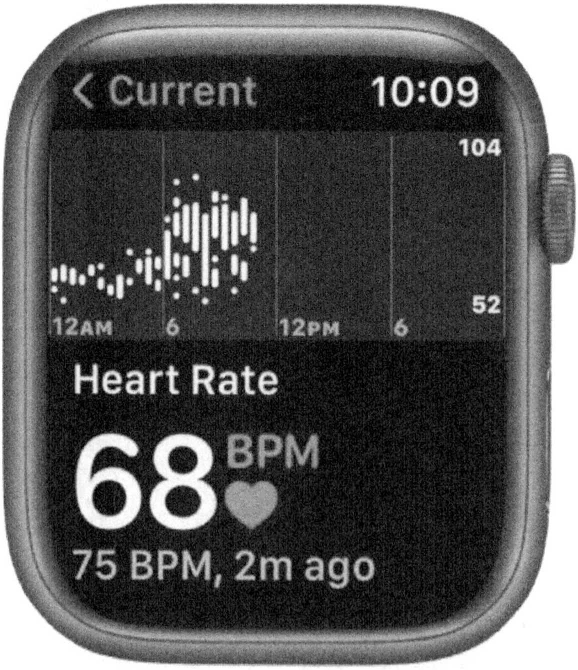

Enter the Heartrate application on your smartwatch to see your heart-rate, rest rate, and average walking rate.

Your smartwatch will continue to measure your heart-rate as long as you are wearing it

View your heart rate data in graphical form

- Enter the Heartrate application on your smartwatch
- Touch the **Current, Walk Average** or **Rest Heart-Rate** button to display your heartrate throughout the day.

To view your heartrate info over a certain period of time, enter the Health application on your phone, touch the **Browse** tab, touch the **Heart** button, and then touch an entry. You can display heartrate info for the last hour, year, month, week, or day.

Activate Heartrate data

By default, your smartwatch tracks your heartrate for the Heartrate application, Reflect, Breathe, & workout sessions. If you have disabled heartrate data, you can follow the directions below to enable it.

- ❖ Enter the Settings application on your smartwatch.
- ❖ Touch Privacy & Security > Health.
- ❖ Touch the **Heart-Rate** button, then activate Heart-Rate.

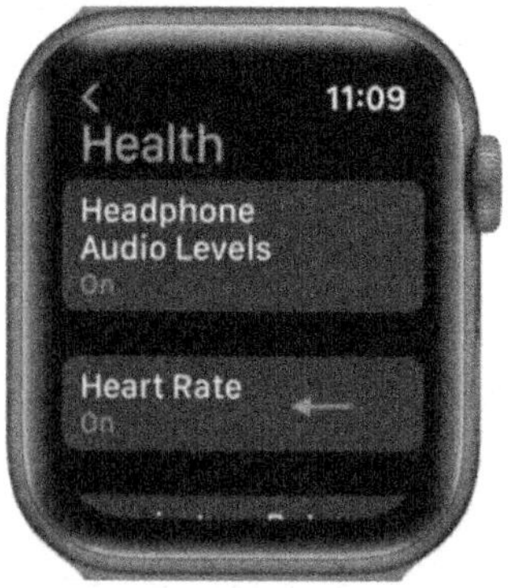

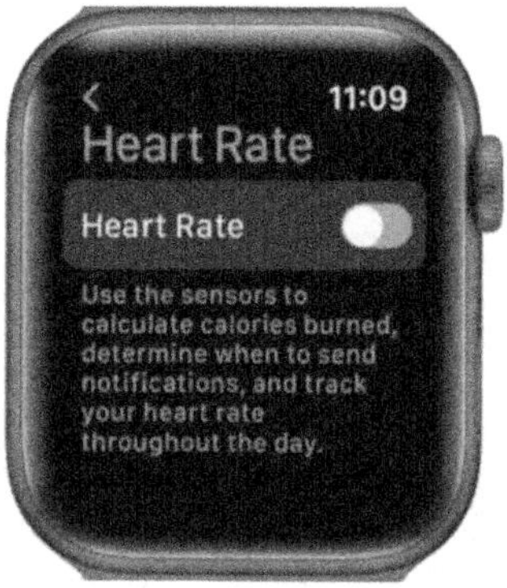

Heart health

Your smartwatch can tune into your heart and send you alerts when something unusual happens. For instance, your smartwatch can alert you if your heart-rate stays above or under a selected threshold after you have been inactive for about Ten minutes.

You can activate this feature the first time you enter the Heartrate application, or at any time thereafter.

You can also get notified when your smartwatch detects a heart rhythm that appears to be AFib.

Get high or low heartrate alerts

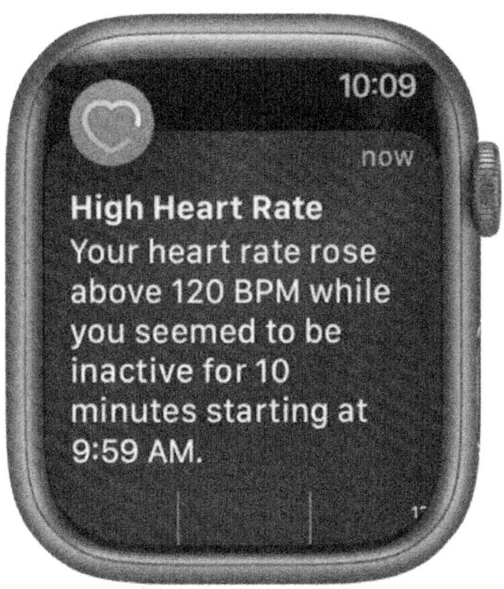

- ❖ Enter the Settings application on your smartwatch, then touch the **Heart** button.

- ❖ Touch the **Low Rate Notification** or the **High Heart Rate Notification** option, then set the heartrate limit.

Or, enter the Watch application on your phone, touch the **My Watch** tab, and then touch the **Heart** button. Touch Low Heart-Rate or High Heart Rate, then set the threshold you want.

Receive alerts for irregular heart rhythms

- ❖ Enter the Settings application on your smartwatch, then touch the **Heart** button.
- ❖ Activate **Irregular Rhythm Notification**.

Or, enter the Watch application on your phone, touch the **My Watch** tab, touch the **Heart** button, then activate **Irregular Rhythms**

Show AFib history

- ❖ If you've been diagnosed with Atrial fibrillation, enter the Health application on your phone, then touch the **Browse** tab.
- ❖ Touch the **Heart** button, scroll to the **Get More From Your Health** section, touch Setup below AFib History, then adhere to the directives on your screen.

- To view your Atrial fibrillation history, enter the Health application, enter the Health application, touch the **Browse** tab, touch the **Heart** button, and then touch AFib History.

Every Monday, if you've worn your smartwatch for about 5 days in the past week (12 hours a day), you can get a message with an estimate of how much time you spent in Atrial fibrillation in the foregoing calendar week

MAIL

Read emails on your smartwatch, then reply with your keyboard, or switch to your iPhone to write a reply.

Read email in a notification

- Lift your wrist when you receive the notification to read the message.
- To dismiss the alert, swipe down from the top of your screen or touch the **Dismiss** button at the bottom of the email.

If you miss an alert, swipe down from the top of your watch face screen to check out all your unread notifications, then touch the notification.

Read your email in the Mail application

- Enter the Mail application on your smartwatch
- Rotate the Digital Crown to scroll through the messages list.
- Touch on of the messages to read it.

❖ To jump to the beginning of a long email, rotate the Digital Crown or tap the top of your display.

Switch to your iPhone

If you receive an email on your smartwatch and you want to read it on your iPhone, adhere to the directives below:

❖ Unlock your phone

- ❖ On a Face ID iPhone, simply swipe up from the lower edge of your screen and stop at the middle to reveal the Application Switcher on your iPhone. (on a Home button iPhone, click the Home button twice quickly to reveal the Application Switcher)
- ❖ Touch the button that shows up at the lower part of your display to enter the Mail application on your iPhone.

Create a message

- ❖ Enter the Mail application on your smartwatch
- ❖ Rotate the Digital Crown to scroll to the top of your watch's screen, then touch the **New Message** button
- ❖ Touch the **Add Contacts** button to add a recipient, touch From to select the account you want to send the email from, touch the **Add Subject** button to create a subject line, and touch the **Create Message** button.
- ❖ Use your finger or the keyboard to type your message.

  You can also touch the Dictate button 🎙 to dictate your message

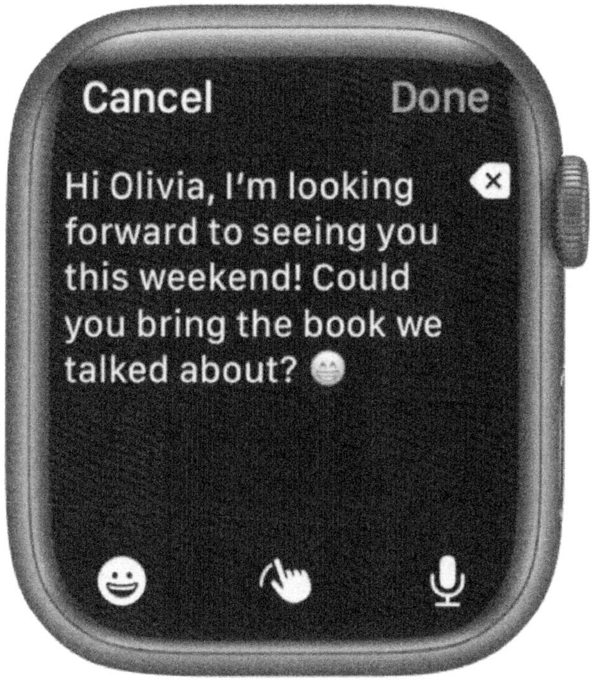
Cancel
Done
Hi Olivia, I'm looking forward to seeing you this weekend! Could you bring the book we talked about?

MAPS

You can use the Maps application on your smartwatch to explore your surroundings and get directions to places.

Search the map

- ❖ Enter the Maps application on your smartwatch
- ❖ Touch the **Search** button, then use the keyboard to type or touch the Dictation icon to dictate.

Find services near you

- ❖ Enter the Maps application on your smartwatch
- ❖ Touch the List icon and then touch a category, like Parking or Fast Food.
- ❖ Touch any of the results and then rotate the Digital Crown to scroll through the info.

❖ Touch the Back button< in the upper left corner of your screen to go back to the results list.

View & search your location and surroundings

❖ Enter the Maps application on your smartwatch
❖ Touch the **Location** button.
❖ To search around your location, touch the More Options icon •••, then touch the **Search Here** button.

Touch the Transits Map to view transit options that are close to you.

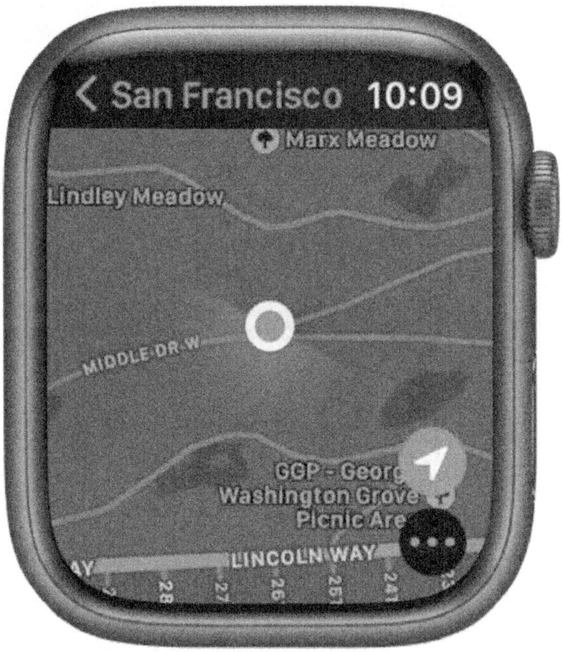

Move & zoom

- Drag a map with one of your fingers to move around it.
- Rotate the Digital Crown to zoom in or out on a map.
  You can also tap your screen twice quickly to zoom in on the place you tap

❖ Touch the Location icon in the lower right part of your screen to return to your current location.

View recent locations

❖ Enter the Maps application on your smartwatch

❖ Scroll down, and then touch any of the locations listed in the Recents section

Get Directions

❖ Enter the Maps application on your smartwatch

❖ Rotate the Digital Crown to go to Favourites, Recents, & Guides.

❖ Touch an entry to receive cycling, transit, walking, & driving directions.

❖ Touch a mode to view recommended routes, then touch one of the routes to start your trip and see an overview of the trip with turns, street names & distance between turns.

Check the upper left corner of your screen to see your approximate arrival time. Touch the arrival time to see how long it will take to arrive.

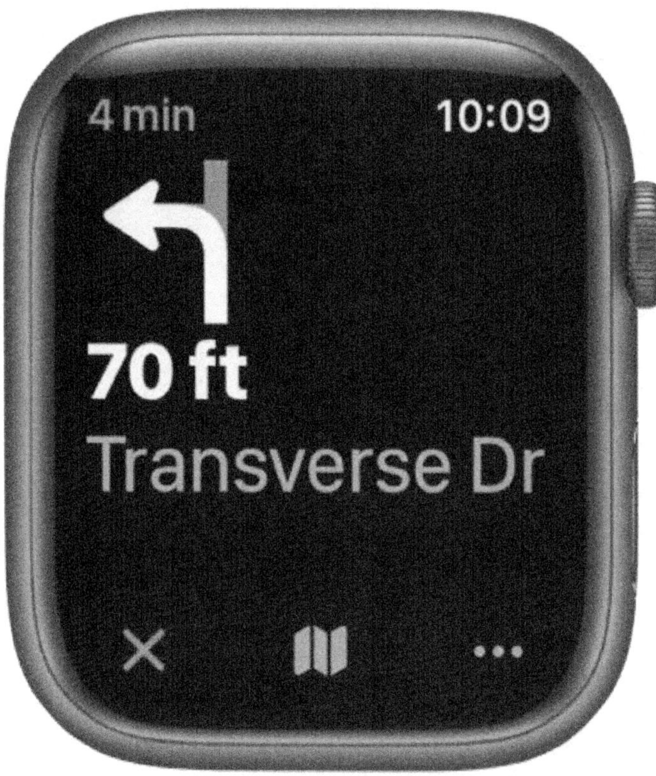

MEDICATIONS

You can manage your medications, supplements & vitamins in the Health application on your phone. You can track your medications and log them with reminders in the Medication application on your smartwatch.

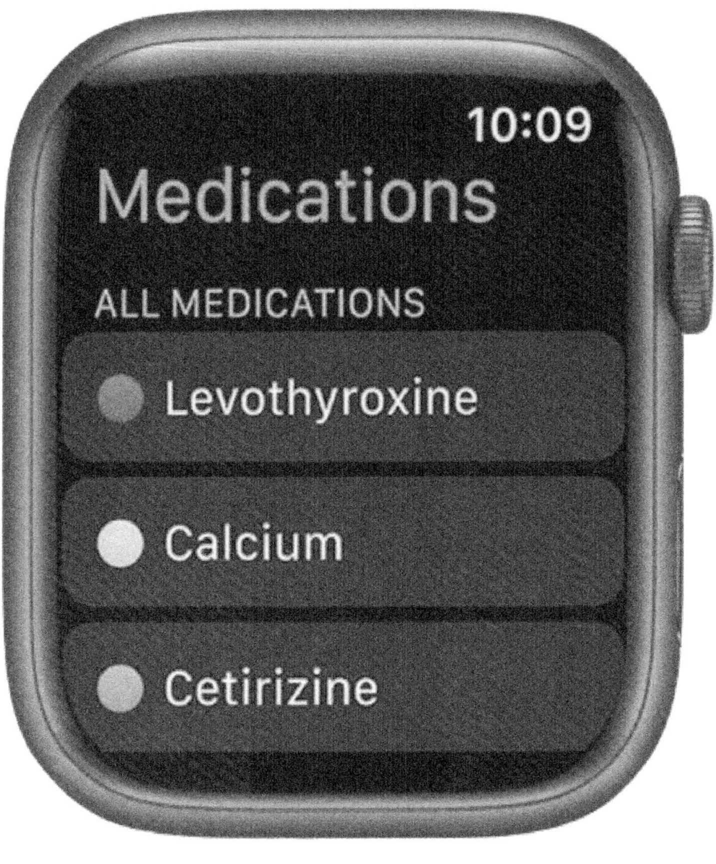

Setup a medication on your phone

- Enter the Health application on your phone, touch the **Browse** tab, and then touch Medications.
- Touch Add Medication.
- Carry out any of the below to identify the medication:
  - Type a name: Touch the search bar, type the name, and then touch the **Add** button.
  - Use your iPhone's camera: Touch the Camera button  beside the search bar then adhere to the directives below.
- Adhere to the directives on your screen to create a visual identifier, create a schedule and help identify possible interactions.

Log your medications

By default, your smartwatch will remind you when it is time to take your medicine according to the schedule you created in the Health application on your phone. Adhere to the directives below to log your medications.

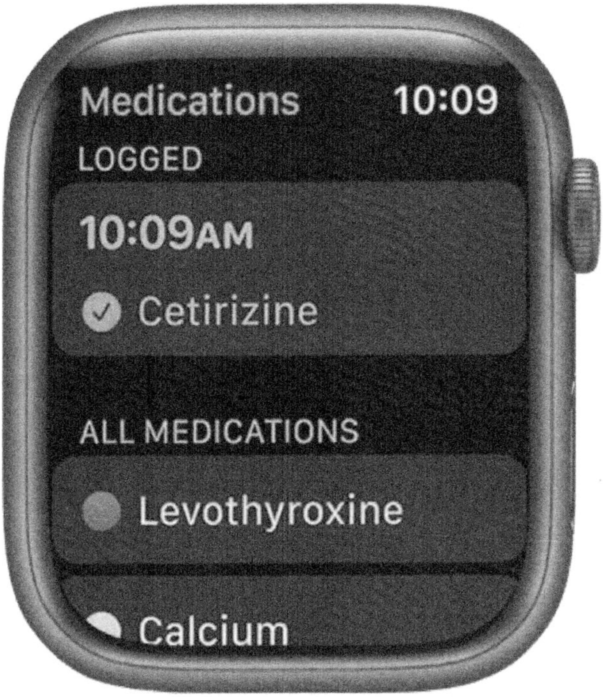

- ❖ If you received an alert to log your medications, touch the notification. Or, enter the Medication application on your smartwatch.
- ❖ Touch your current medication schedule, for instance, your morning medication.
- ❖ Touch Log All as Taken.
  Your smartwatch records the dosage, how many units were taken, and when you took the medicine.

- To register individual medications, scroll, touch a medication in the Your Medications section, and then touch the **Log** button.
  The name of the medication and the time you logged will appear in the Logged section.
- To change a logged medication status, touch it, touch the **Skipped** or the **Taken** button, then touch the **Done** button.

To see the log and your medication history on your phone, enter the Health application, touch the **Browse** tab, then touch the **Medications** button.

MEMOJI

With the Memoji application, you can create your Memoji - pick skin colour, glasses, head wear, etc. You can design many Memojis for different moods.

Create Memoji

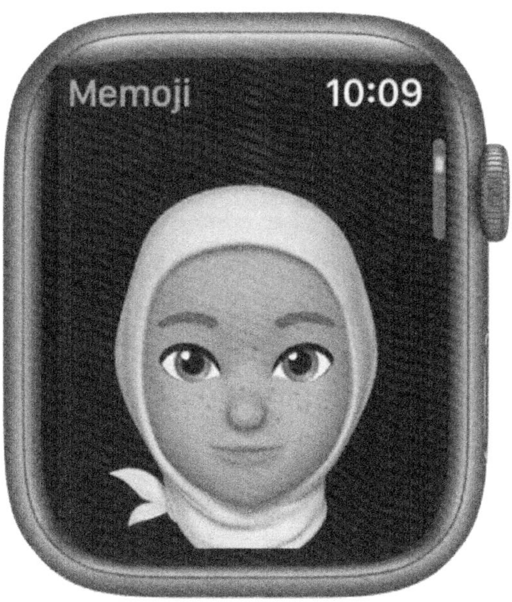

- Enter the Memoji application on your smartwatch.

- If this is your first time using the Memoji application, touch the **Get Started** button.
  If you're creating a Memoji before, scroll down and then touch the Add Memoji icon ⊕ to add a new memoji.
- Touch the features you want and scroll the Digital Crown to select the options you want for the Memoji. Adding features like hairstyles & glasses will bring your character to life.
- Touch the **Done** button to the Memoji to your Memoji collections.

Edit, Duplicate Memoji & more

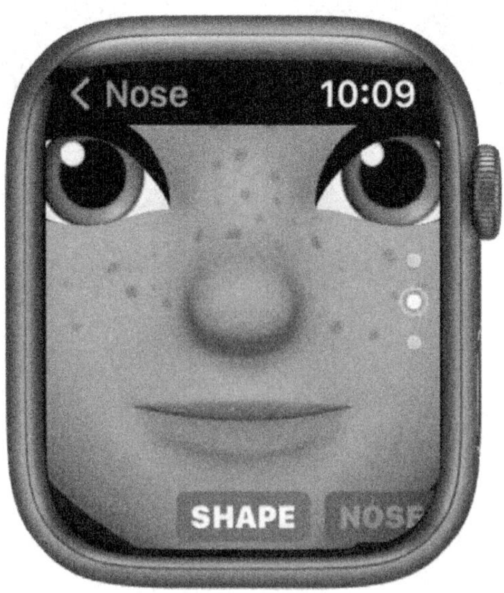

Enter the Memoji application on your Smartwatch, touch one of your Memoji, and choose an option:

- Edit a Memoji: Touch features like headwear & eyes, then rotate the Digital Crown to select a variation.
- Duplicate a Memoji: Scroll down, then touch the **Duplicate** button.
- Create a Memoji watch face: Scroll down, then touch the **Create Watch Face** button.
  Go back to your watch face, swipe left to check out your new Memoji watch face.
- Delete a Memoji: Scroll down, then touch the **Delete** button

MINDFULNESS

The Mindfulness application on your smartwatch recommends taking a few minutes each day to focus, & connect with your breathing.

Begin a meditation or breathing session

Enter the Mindfulness application, then carry out any of the below:

- Breathe: Touch the **Breathe** button, breathe in slowly as the animation increases, then breathe out as it gets smaller.

❖ Reflect: Touch the **Reflect** button, read the topic, focus, and then touch the **Begin** button.

To end a Breathe or Reflect session before it completes, swipe to the right, then touch the **End** button.

Set the duration of a session

❖ Enter the Mindfulness application

❖ Touch the More Options icon •••, touch the **Duration** button, and then select the duration.
You can choose between 1 minute & 5 minutes.

Change mindfulness settings

Enter the Settings application on your smartwatch, touch Mindfulness, then carry out any of the below:

❖ Set reminders: In the Reminders section, activate or deactivate Start of Day & End of

Day; touch the **Add Reminder** button to create more reminders.

- Receive or stop weekly summary: Enable or disable Weekly Summary.
- Silent mindfulness reminder: Activate the **Mute for Today** feature
- Get new meditations: Activate the **Add a New Meditation to Watch** feature to download new meditations when your smartwatch is charging. The Meditations you have completed will be erased from your watch automatically.

NOISE

The Noise application on your smartwatch measures the sound level in your environment. When your smartwatch notices that the decibel level is high enough to affect your hearing it can alert you with a tap on your wrist.

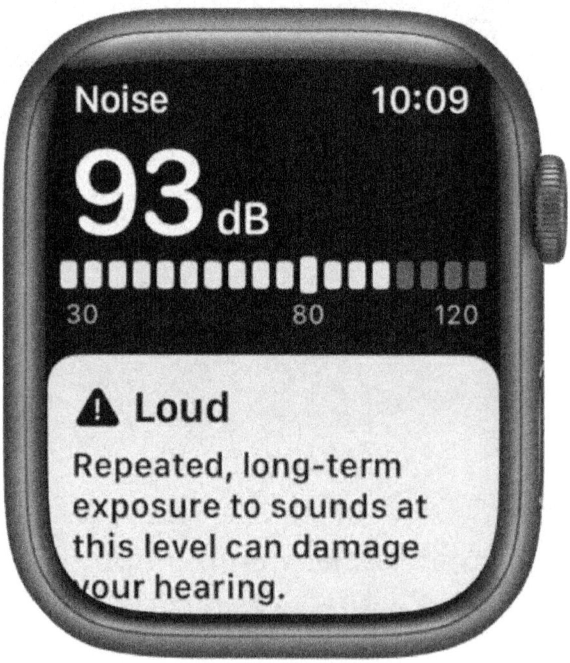

Setup the Noise application

- ❖ Enter the Noise application on your smartwatch.

- ❖ Touch the **Enable** button to activate monitoring.
- ❖ In the future, launch the Noise application to measure the ambient noise around you.

Receive noise notifications

- ❖ Enter the Settings application on your smartwatch.
- ❖ Touch Noise > Noise Notifications, and then select any of the settings.

Deactivate noise measuring

- ❖ Enter the Settings application on your smartwatch.
- ❖ Touch Noise >Environmental Sound Measurement, then deactivate **Measure Sound**.

View a noise notification details

You can receive a notification on your phone from your smartwatch when the noise around you gets to a level that could affect your hearing

To see the details of an alert, adhere to the directives below:

- Enter the Health application on your phone, and then touch the Summary tab in the lower left part of your screen.
- Touch the notification close to the upper part of your screen, and then touch the **Show More Data** button.

PHONE

Answer a phone call

When you hear a call notification, lift your hand to see who is calling.

- ❖ Touch the red Reject button to decline the call.
- ❖ Touch the green Accept button to answer the call.
- ❖ Answer the call with your iPhone or send an SMS instead: Touch the More Options icon •••

, then tap any of the Options. If you touched the **Answer on your iPhone** option, the call will be put on hold and the caller will hear a repeated sound until you answer on the paired phone.

If you cannot find your phone, Long-press the bottom of your watch's screen, swipe up to reveal the Controls Centre, then touch the Ping iPhone button on your smartwatch

While you are on a call

While on a call you can carry out any of the below:

- Transfer a call from your smartwatch to your phone: while having a conversation on a call in your smartwatch, unlock your phone, then touch the green button or bar at the upper part of your screen.
- Change the call volume: Rotate the Digital Crown. Touch the Mute button to mute your end (for example, if you are on a conference call).
- Enter more numbers during a call: Touch the More Options icon, touch the **Keypad** button, and then tap the numbers.

- Switch the call to an audio device: Touch the More Options icon •••, then select a device.

Listen to a voicemail

If the caller leaves a voicemail, you'll get a notification - touch Play in the notification to listen to it. To listen to it some other time, enter the Phone application on your smartwatch, then touch Voicemail.

Make a call

- Enter the Phone application on your smartwatch.
- Touch the **Contacts** button, then rotate the Digital Crown to scroll through the list.
- Touch the contact you plan on calling and then touch the Phone button.
- Touch the **Face-Time Audio** button to make a FaceTime voice call or touch a phone number.
- Rotate the Digital Crown to change the volume level during a call.

Enter a number on your smartwatch

- Enter the Phone application on your smartwatch.
- Touch the **Keypad** button, type the phone number, then touch the Call button .

CONTROL APPLE TV WITH APPLE WATCH

Your smartwatch can serve as a remote for your Apple TV when connected to the same WiFi network.

Connect your Apple Watch to Apple TV

If your phone isn't connected to the WiFi network that your Apple TV is on, connect it now, then adhere to the directives below:

- Enter the Remote application on your smartwatch.
- Touch your Apple TV. If it’s not on the list, touch the **Add Device** button.
- On your Apple TV, enter the Settings application> Remote & Devices > Remotes App & Devices, then choose Apple Watch.
- Insert the pass-code displayed on your smartwatch.

When you see the pairing icon beside your Apple Watch, it means your watch can now control your Apple TV.

Use your Apple Watch to control your Apple TV

Ensure your Apple TV is awake, then adhere to the directives below:

- Enter the Remote application  on your smartwatch.
- Touch your Apple TV, then swipe right, left, down, or up to navigate through your Apple TV menu options.

- Touch to select the selected item.
- Touch the Pause/Play button to pause or play what you are watching.
- Touch the Menu key to go back, or long-press the Menu button to go back to the main menu.

To launch the screensaver, go to the upper -left corner of your Apple TV's Home screen, and then touch the Menu button.

Unpair & remove Apple TV

1. On your Apple TV, enter the Settings application> Remote & Devices > Remotes App & Devices
2. Touch your Apple Watch in the Remote App section, and then touch Unpair this Device.
3. Enter the Remote application on your smartwatch and when you see the "lost connections" message, touch the **Remove** button.

SLEEP

With the Sleep application, you can create a sleep schedule to help you reach your sleep goals. Put on your smartwatch to bed, and it can track how much time you spend in each stage of sleep—REM, Core, & Deep—as well as when you wake up. When you wake up, enter the Sleep application to learn how much sleep you've had and what your sleep patterns have been over the past 14 days.

You can create multiple schedules, for instance, one schedule for weekends and another sleep schedule for weekdays.

Setup sleep

- Enter the Sleep application on your smartwatch.
- Adhere to the directives on your display.

You can also enter the Health application on your phone, touch the Browse tab, touch the **Sleep** button, and then touch the **Get Started** button in the Setup Sleep section.

Change or turn off the next wakeup alarm

- Enter the Sleep application on your smartwatch.
- Touch your present bedtime
- To set a new wakeup time, touch the wakeup time, rotate the Digital Crown to set a time, then touch the Confirm icon .

Turn off Alarm if you do not want your smartwatch to wake you up in the morning.

You can also enter the Health application on your phone, touch the Browse tab, touch the **Sleep** button, and then touch the **Edit** button under Your Schedule to adjust your schedule

This change only applies to your next wakeup alarm, after which your normal routine will resume.

Change or add a sleep schedule

- Enter the Sleep application on your smartwatch.
- Touch Full Schedule, then carry out one of the below:

  - Touch the current sleep schedule to make changes to it
  - Touch the **Add Schedule** button to add a sleep schedule.
  - Change your sleep target: Touch Sleep Goals, then set your sleep duration

- Make changes to wind-down time: Touch the **Wind Down** button, then set how long you want the Sleep Focus to be on before you fall asleep.

❖ Carry out any of the below:

- Set your schedule days: Touch your schedule, then touch Active On. Select days, then touch <.
- Change your wakeup time & bedtime: Touch your schedule, touch Wakeup or Bedtime, rotate the Digital Crown to set a new time, and then touch the Confirm icon .
- Set alarm options: Touch your schedule, then enable or disable Alarm and touch Sounds and Haptic to select an alarm sound.
- Delete or cancel a schedule: Touch your schedule, then touch the **Delete Schedule** button at the lower part of your display to remove a schedule, or touch the **Cancel** button at the upper part of your display to cancel creating a new schedule.

View your recent sleep history

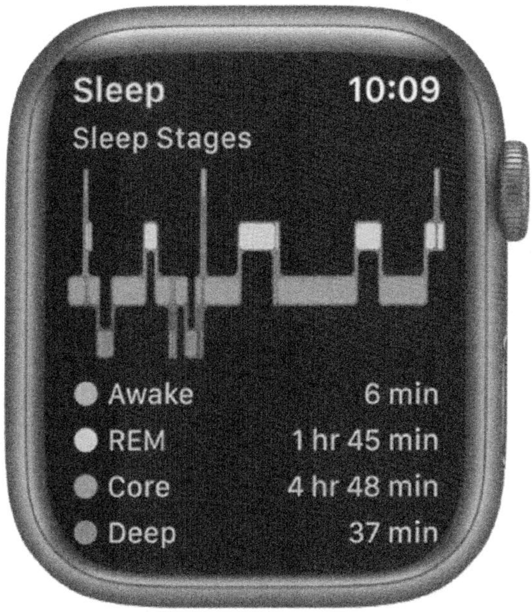

- Enter the Sleep application on your smartwatch.
- Scroll down to check out how much sleep you had the night before, how long you spent in each sleep phase and your sleep average over the past 14 days.

Check your sleep respiratory rate

Your smartwatch can monitor your breathing rate while you sleep, which can give you more insight into your overall well-being. After putting on your smartwatch to bed, adhere to the directives below:

- ❖ Enter the Health application on your phone, touch the Browse tab, and then touch the **Respiratory** button.
- ❖ Touch Respiratory Rate, then touch Show Respiratory Rate Data.

  The sleep entry will show the range of your respiratory rate when you were asleep.

Track your nightly wrist temperature

When worn to bed every night, your smartwatch can keep track of your wrist temperature changes each night to provide insight into your well-being.

Setup wrist temperature tracking

- ❖ Turn on Track Sleep with Apple Watch (in the Sleep application)

  Or, enter the Watch application on your phone, touch **My Watch,** touch the **Sleep** button, then touch **Track Sleep with Apple Watch** to activate this feature.

- To set a temperature profile, make sure Sleep Focus is turned on, then wear your smartwatch while you sleep.
  Wrist temperature info will be available after 5 nights.

Note: The temperature of your body fluctuates naturally and may differ from night to night due to several variables. Wrist temperature can also be affected by external factors, such as your sleep environment.

Review your wrist temperature

- Enter the Health application on your phone, then touch the Browse tab
- Touch Body Measurement, then touch Wrist Temperature
- Touch a point in the chart to see sample details

Disable wrist temperature tracking

- Enter the Watch application on your phone.
- Touch the My Watch tab, touch the Privacy button, and then disable wrist Temperature.

APPLE PAY

Apple Pay offers an easy & safe way to make payments on your smartwatch.

Add a card to your watch with your phone

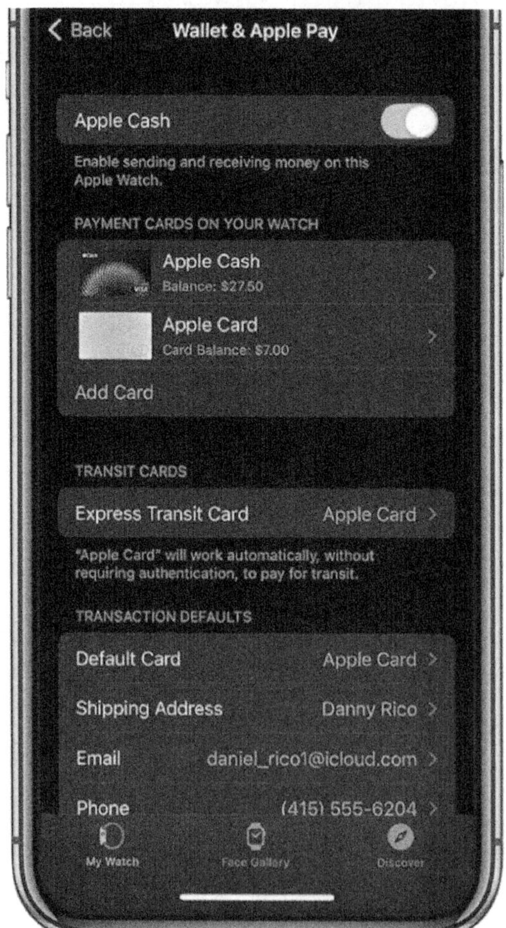

- Enter the Watch application on your phone.
- Touch the My Watch tab, then touch the **Wallet and Apple Pay** button
- Touch Add Card, and adhere to the directives on your screen.

Your card provider may ask for more steps to verify your information.

Add a card on your smartwatch

You can add transit, debit, or credit cards right on your smartwatch.

- Enter the Wallet application on your smartwatch.
- Scroll down, then touch the **Add Card** button.
- Select Transit Card, Apple Account, Credit, or Debit Card; then adhere to the directives on your screen.

Select your default card

- Enter the Watch application on your phone.
- Touch the **My Watch** tab, touch Wallet and Apple Pay, touch Default card, then choose one of your cards.

Rearrange your payment cards

Enter the Wallet application on your smartwatch, long-press a card, then move it to a new location by dragging it there.

Remove a card

- Enter the Wallet application on your smartwatch.
- Touch to select the card
- Scroll, and then touch the **Remove** button.

Change your default transaction information

You can change transaction info—including e-mail, default card, number, & shipping address.

- Enter the Watch application on your phone.
- Touch the **My Watch** tab, touch Wallet and Apple Pay, then scroll down to display Transaction Defaults.
- Touch an item to change it.

Pay for items in a store with your smartwatch

- ❖ Click the side button twice quickly.
- ❖ Scroll to select a card.
- ❖ Take your smartwatch very close to the contactless card reader, and make sure the screen is facing the reader.

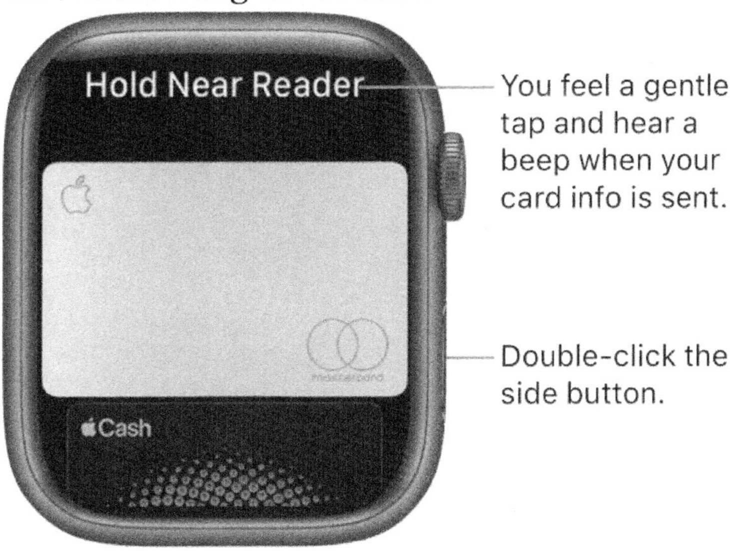

You will feel a soft tap & hear a beep when the payment info has been sent.

You will get a notification in the Notifications Centre when the transaction is confirmed.

Pay for items in an application

- When shopping in an application on your smartwatch, select the Apple Pay option when checking out.
- Go through your shipping, payment, & billing details, then click the side button twice quickly to pay for the items with your smartwatch.

Printed in Great Britain
by Amazon

10616074R00169